BREAKTHROUGH TO PEAK PERFORMANCE

by Jim Steele, Martin Coburn and Colin Hiles

BREAKTHROUGH TO PEAK PERFORMANCE
by Jim Steele, Martin Coburn and Colin Hiles

Copyright ©1999 by Speakers International Corporate Development Ltd.
Publisher ℗ The Catalyst Group
First edition 1999

ILLUSTRATIONS BY
Charlie Edwards

COVER DESIGN BY
Charlie Edwards
Casey Hargreaves

PUBLISHED BY
The Catalyst Group
1 Berghem Mews
Blythe Road
London W14 0HN
http//:www.catalyst-group.com
Tel:0171 603 7779 Fax:0171 603 2220

A catalogue for this book is available from the British Library
ISBN 0 9535557 0 4

Printed and bound in Great Britian
by Redwood Books, Trowbridge. Wiltshire

Dedication

This book is dedicated to the 100th monkey in all of us.

F O R E W O R D

Jim Steele, Martin Coburn and Colin Hiles are a group of highly talented motivational and inspirational people who work as coaches for Speakers International.

Speakers International visit companies and organisations where they meet and enthuse groups of people. Jim, Martin and Colin will all tell you that they see their task not so much as the motivation of the people they meet, but rather as coaching them to realise their own potential.

Their whole philosophy is based on an interactive participation and that same philosophy pervades this book. If you, the readers, are not prepared to play your part, you will not gain the maximum benefit from it. You will find yourself involved in role-play, in exercising your imagination, in writing things down, in giving honest answers to searching questions and challenges.

If you want to gain the maximum benefit, it is important that you are prepared to play your part and to take the necessary action.

Jim, Martin and Colin would not have been able to complete 'Breakthrough to Peak Performance' without the ever conscious help of Los Haward as creative consultant and indeed my final edit - a task which in itself brought challenges to my own experience.

If success could be handed to you on a plate, it would not be worth having. At the very least you must be ready to pick up your own metaphorical knife and fork and dig in.

David Hannon
EDITOR

CONTENTS

P E A K

P E R F O R M A N C E

E very person has potential. Some will say that that potential has no limits other than the limit of one's own ambition. But every person is different; each person is an individual.

Performance can be improved by training. Not only the physical body can be trained. The mind can be trained. Attitude can be trained. Expectations can be trained.

Peak Performance is the fulfilment of potential. It can only be achieved by reaching maximum fitness of body and mind, of attitude and expectation.

A Peak Performer is fit for any challenge, is mentally equipped to meet the challenge, approaches the challenge knowing that it can be met and certain that it will be completed.

Those four conditions are closely inter-related. If any one of them is allowed to falter, the whole will falter.

Peak Performers are genuinely ready, willing and able.

I N T R O D U C T I O N

Who do you think you are?

Have you ever asked yourself that question? Most of us have heard it at one time or another, asked by somebody else. When that has happened, the tone has often been aggressive, negative and sarcastic. The question has really been '*How dare you presume to be taking your present attitude?*'

That is not the question we are asking now. It is not the question we are suggesting that you ask yourself. In both cases it is a genuine enquiry asked in a caring and genuinely interested tone.

Who exactly do you think you are?

Whatever the answer you give yourself, you are probably right, because quite simply we tend to become the person we think we are. For most of us this is a totally unconscious process since we have never actually thought of asking the question of ourselves at all in the first place!

Once we accept the validity of this idea that we tend to become the person we think we are, the time has come to take the obvious next step and to ask another question instead.

Who do you want to be?

If the answers to these last two questions are different, then you have identified the fundamental purpose of this book. For those who have two differing answers, we will supply the tools that we know you will need and which we believe will make it possible for you to close the gap between them.

Return for a moment to the original question put to you in that aggressive and sarcastic manner. The probability is that you heard it in your early formative years when you were young and in the middle of the time of your most conspicuous growth and development. At a time when we are developing our own per-sonalities, surely we need most support and not a dismissive slapping down.

Our society likes to have its own rules and to have them based on accepted standards or beliefs. They may come from religion. They may come from 'authority'. They are designed to keep everyone in their own place and to prevent them from rocking the boat.

Centuries of experience have made it obvious that an obedient and subservient society is easily managed. The logical consequence is to instil that obedience, that subservience, that acceptance of the rules from the earliest stages of life.

No intelligent person would question the positive and constructive values of much of our inherited beliefs and traditional standards. At the same time, no intelligent person can look back over the centuries and deny that nearly every rev-olutionary change in human development has been brought about by people who were prepared to ask questions about what everyone else accepted.

The classical example is the Copernican revolution. It was Copernicus who had the visionary audacity to suggest that the planets orbited the sun. Of course at the time everyone knew and believed that the sun and the stars and everything else revolved around the earth!

Every so often, such a sudden shift in the state of affairs is caused by just such a reversal of the previous model.

In this book we are going to pursue our own reversal which involves seeing the individual as being responsible for making his world happen instead of the world making the individual.

Over the centuries, institutionalised religions have laid down rules and patterns of behaviour. Occasionally these have been enlightening and positive. Few could quarrel with '*Love your neighbour*'! More often rules have been inhibiting with their '*Thou shalt not*' thesis and their insistence on strict behavioural patterns.

More recently the flock of - 'isms' - Fascism, Communism, Capitalism, Socialism - although opposed to each other on almost all other fronts, agree on one point. The individual is merely a cog on the wheel. The personal must be subordinate to the collective. In every case, only a few stand to benefit from the system and it is in their interest to keep things that way. The mood of despair and negativity which that produces is deeply reflected in much of the art and intellectual history of the nineteenth and twentieth centuries.

All these ideologies have a common pattern made up of three elements - a Philosophy, a Passion and a Plan. If we are to compete with them, we must meet them on their own ground. We must have our own alternative Philosophy, our own driving Passion and our own Plan to make them truly effective.

Plato said in the language of his day that any blueprint for the best requires a good look at the worst. His student, Aristotle went further: '*In framing an ideal we may assume what we wish but should avoid impossibilities.*' That is true, but what was clearly impossible for Aristotle is in many cases an every day situation for us.

For Aristotle it was impossible to travel at fifty miles an hour. Indeed as recently as the early years of the nineteenth century, people seriously believed that travelling at such a speed on the new-fangled railways could injure your health and even threaten your life! As for man walking on the Moon, such a concept was not on Aristotle's map of reality - and he was very much a forward thinker.

Today we are in a position to realise that we have never made a map of life that is as big, as beautiful, as creative, courageous, elegant, generous or amazing as the available territory itself. We have come a long way from a world as flat as a plate whose edge you would surely fall over if you sailed too far out to sea.

Experience of recent years underlines that inherited attitudes and inhibitions must not be allowed to embed our mind-set in stone. Every one of us has the potential to move on. Every one of us must be ready to accept the biggest of all new beliefs - the belief that it lies within each of us to make the difference that will make the difference!

That is the basis for our ideology. In pursuit of the 'Breakthrough' in the title of this book, we will be driving towards a new attitude. We have a Philosophy. We have a Passion. We have a Plan. We have an attitude.

THIS IS A BOOK WITH ATTITUDE!

BREAKTHROUGH
TO
PEAK PERFORMANCE

Part One

PERSONAL LEADERSHIP

P R E P A R E

I n the Introduction we identified the two questions. 'Who do you think you are?' and 'Who do you want to be?'

The revolutionary thought which we brought to your attention is that the answer to the second question has the potential to become a self-fulfilling prophecy.

You can become what you want to be once you know what that is and once you have learnt how to achieve it. One of the best things about the new experimental science of Peak Performance is that it is a very 'hands-on' business. It is more interested in making things happen than in talking about what it might be like if things did happen.

For that reason you will find many practical elements in what this book has to say.

Look at the picture. Do you notice anything unusual? The conductor and the musicians are all the same person. In case you have not guessed, that person is you! Each of the instruments represents an aspect which we will help you develop. The aspect may be your motivation, your beliefs or your communication skills. Remember you are the conductor. You will only make great music if you give great leadership.

You need to make the decision to set out on this journey. Your self-development must be under the authority of your own personal leadership.

If you are a musician you will understand the orchestral metaphor. Even if you are not musical you will recognise the leadership of the conductor.

Everyone, musical or not, recognises the idea of a tool kit. As you work to 'Breakthrough to Peak Performance' you are going to learn how to use a variety of tools. As you follow the exercises in this book you will master the necessary skills and build up an effective collection. Some of the tools are simply the application of common sense. Some of them are quite advanced pieces of applied technology and have fancy names.

You are going to learn how to control your psychological focus. This will allow you to control your position on what we call the Performance Scale using techniques with names such as

- Memory Management
- Mental Rehearsal
- Scramble
- Disassociation

You are going to learn the benefits of a positive physiology and how to manage your internal dialogue. Talking to yourself is not always the first sign of madness!

You are going to learn how to re-design your belief system through rejecting and selecting reference points, through opening your thinking to new possibilities, through re-wiring your pain/pleasure associations and through using a technique called 're-framing.'

You are going to learn how to achieve rapport with other people using **Mirroring and Matching** and how to make communication really effective using the Precision Model.

You will learn how to monitor your own behaviour through mindfulness and self-separation.

There will be other things!

When you have learnt them all you will be ready for whatever the task may be, whether as an accomplished craftsman or as conductor of your own orchestra.

The first thing you will have to do is to apply for the job of being the conductor. Since it is your orchestra, you will be applying to yourself for the job. You might assume straight away that you have got it. On the other hand, it might be worth having a look at yourself as you are at the moment and asking yourself would you give that person such an important job! There is so much to learn.

However, once you stand on the podium you will be able to see all the instruments and how they relate to each other. You will know why you are using them and as you qualify fully for the conductor's job you will lead them together to create the symphony of your new identity.

You may hesitate before picking up the baton but that move is essential to success. Taking action is always the master key. As you build up the different skills and bring them together you will realise the importance of their combination. Of course they can be used separately and have their individual impacts.

What Peak Performers find out is the way in which they do inter-relate so that they enhance each other's powers.

Look back at the list of the things you are going to learn and you will realise that with practice and application they will give you power over your own behaviour and therefore over your level of achievement.

Of course there are no guarantees in this business. It would not be an adventure if there were. Everything would be totally pre-planned and there would be no doubts about the outcome.

But with all the skills you will learn, you will have so much power available for our adventure together that we already have cause for celebration.

Peak Performers need to be adventurous, resourceful, flexible, ready to take opportunities when they are on offer and also generous, giving and outgoing with abundance.

One of the key elements in this book is that there is a significant connection between us and the world we live in. We are not working or living in a vacuum. If you put **yourself** together you begin to put the **world** together.

> A father wanted to keep his young son busy while he got on with some work. He found a complex picture of the world in an old magazine so he tore it into small pieces and challenged the boy to reassemble it. You might call it a home-made jigsaw puzzle.
>
> Just a short while later his son came back with the picture completely restored. 'How did you manage that so quickly?' his father asked. 'It was easy,' said the boy, 'there was a picture of a man on the other side of the page. When I put the man together, I had put the world together as well!'

That is a nice example of the same idea. It means being prepared to go for the **'inside-out'** approach. Start with yourself and the world will follow. That is our first lesson. Take control and become the architect of your own destiny.

Think about that. If you are going to take responsibility for mastering your own motivation, rebuilding your belief system and taking the lead in communicating with others, you are not going to hand over the issue of your personal destiny to outside forces. You are going to choose to lead yourself.

Where you go is up to you.

You will only be truly free if you decide to take freedom for yourself and you must be prepared to accept that taking freedom involves accepting the personal responsibility that goes with it.

Your destiny will not be decided by some kind of existential travel agent. Your outcome is your own. Of course if you decide not to make a decision, someone else will certainly make it for you. Remember, every decision has a destination, even the decision not to make a decision!

The same rule applies with the kind of success you achieve. The point here is that it will be the result of realising what success means to you. The new 'you' will not be ready to settle for pre-packaged, off-the-shelf symbols of success designed by politicians, businessmen or leaders of religious cults. You will demand your own kind of success which may well be quite different from the established clichés of fame and fortune.

That may be your choice. If it is, that is fine. All that matters is that it should be the result of your own independent decision. It is not our job to set your target. Our challenge is to help you to reach yours, whatever it may be.

All the work we are going to do together must be based on the fact that you assume direct control of your own destiny. It is you who decides what that destiny will be and how you are going to reach it.

You will have your orchestra. What music will you play? You will have your tool kit. What structure will you build? Perhaps you will end up with a powerful vehicle where you are at the controls. At every junction the choice of route will be in your hands.

V A L U E S

Before we can make intelligent decisions about the direction in which we plan to go, we need to have some idea of the relative importance of various aspects of our lives. In the chart below we have listed seven areas which we believe most people would consider significant.

AREA	A	B	C
Health and Energy			10
Loving Relationships			10
Social			10
Financial			10
Career			10
Personal Development			10
Peace of Mind			10

Exercise 1   Personality Profile
Make your own chart adding any areas you would choose.

Now think back to five years ago. Assess your level on a scale from 1 to 10 for each area and enter the figure in column A. You may find this difficult but be as honest and as accurate as you can.

When you have completed the first column, take an equally honest look at your situation as you believe it is now. As before, compare your present levels against the 10's in column C which represents the potential which you believe you ought to be achieving. Once again, fill in the figures, this time in column B.

In case you are surprised by the results, you should know that it is very unlikely that the figures will be the same in both cases.

You can use these figures to create what we call your Personality Profile.

Take the figures in Column A and create a bar graph from them. If you draw a continuous line across the tops of the columns, it will have its ups and downs. Now, with a different coloured pen or pencil, do the same thing on the same diagram using the figures from column B. As you will have guessed, the two top lines are unlikely to be the same.

In the following illustration, we have deliberately left out any identification of the columns - because we do not want to tempt you into using our picture for comparison with your own or using it to help you make judgements which are your own responsibility!

The two top lines can be seen as giving varying pictures and representations of your personality profile. In their own way, you could think of them as pictures of the road surface which you are using to drive along in the 'car' of your life.

PERSONALITY PROFILES

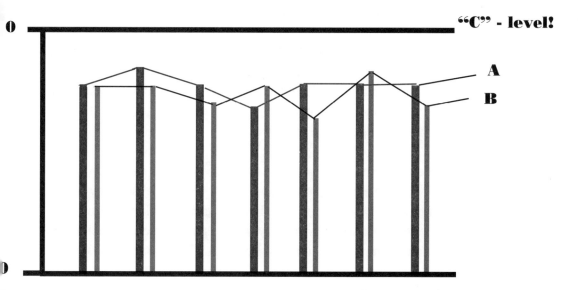

If there are too many humps and hollows in the profile, you are going to have a bumpy ride - unless you do something to avoid the potholes which you have identified or you do something to make the road surface more even by bringing the various elements of your profile into better alignment.

From your own experience, you will know how much more comfortable the ride can be when the road surface is in perfect and smoothly even condition. In your case it would be so if you could bring those achievement levels all up to the 10's which you yourself have decided to use as the standards for your own judgement.

Go back for a moment to the figures which you entered in columns A and B. Think about the changes and differences which you may have noticed. Some may be greater than others. In some areas it may look as if your level has gone down. When that happened, how did you react? Did you see it immediately as failure?

You need never do so again.

What you have in front of you is not failure, it is **information feedback**. What is more it is very instructive feedback. The past need not equal the future and the future is in your own hands. If you do not like it, change it. As you read on, you will find advice on how change can be achieved.

When you study the patterns you have created you may decide that you have over-valued some areas. You are absolutely free to change their importance so that the various values are more in line with each other. As long as that is a conscious decision and not an attempt to diminish a challenge, that is fine.

Ideally things will be in alignment.

Your actions will be in line with your goals and your goals will be in line with your beliefs and values. Of course it is important that our goals and beliefs make sense together. If your goal is to own a big house but you believe that you cannot make enough money to buy it, you will end up disillusioned!

The same idea applies to goals and values. If you value world peace but your goal is to make your fortune selling armaments, you are going to experience serious internal conflicts. Alignment is the key.

To find out where we are at, we need to do some more analysis.

You are the only person who can work out your own situation. It is your responsibility to carry out a check on your own status. You will need to play your part in the next exercise. The exercise comes in the form of four steps. Take them in order.

Exercise 2   Goal Scoring
Step One

Think about the goals you are pursuing now. Imagine them being achieved. Now pick the ones that seem most important. Do you realise that these identify your particular desired future? Write the three or four most important ones each at the head of a column on one of the back pages of this book.

Step Two

Consider each goal in turn. See it, hear it, feel it, experience it as a goal which you actually own. Now ask yourself *'What do I really value about this goal?'* For example, if the goal is to travel widely, the values might be 'fun' or 'learning' or 'adventure' or something else. Under each goal write down the values you associate with it.

Step Three

You will now have a list of values which your own choice of goals has identified as being important to you. They are all there for you to see. Now ask yourself *'What is most important to me about **all** these values?'*

Knowing that most important underlying value is crucial to understanding yourself. The answers to the questions explain how your values were motivating you, influencing every action.

Step Four

When you have identified the underlying value and thought about it you will begin to understand the benefit of having that knowledge. You will have put your finger on your own central motivation. At the bottom of your lists write down that core value. Highlight it. Remember it. To help you remember, transfer it into your diary or your organiser where you will see it regularly.

When you see it, ask yourself *'How often am I experiencing this value?'* If we do not live in accordance with our most important values we experience disappointment, emptiness or even depression.

All our goals, all our dreams and desires are nothing but the vehicles for fulfilling our values. They are the symbols we can see in front of us. If we become disconnected from our values we lose motivation. It is inevitable. When we lose sight of where we are going, we become experts at the art of wasting time! It is only later that we may wonder where the time has gone.

How much time have we got? Statisticians will tell us the details of the hours we spend queueing, or shopping, or eating, or sleeping or on any of the other myriad activities we all perform.

One thing is certain. Each piece of time taken up reduces the amount left. Whatever that may be, it is not enough to allow for the kind of aimless drifting which we indulge in when our lives are **not** being lived in accordance with our values!

Is there anything we can do to help ourselves to be sure that we **do** live in this way? We believe there is. Suppose, for example, that one of our core values is security. We may take that further by believing that security will follow -

- If the mortgage is paid off.
- If everyone likes us.
- If the job is safe.
- If our partner is going to stay
  with us for the rest of our life.

Many of those beliefs are outside our own control and for that reason they may lead to insecurity if they fall down. But we can set up the game to be sure of winning by designing rules or beliefs that make it easy for us to meet our values. Go back for a moment to the list of requirements above which we thought would lead to security. Replace them with new ideas. Try these.

- Any time we are paying off the mortgage.
- Any time we can recognise that we have
  acted as a true friend.
- Any time we take action to learn
  new skills at work.
- Any time we take steps to improve
  relationships with our partners.

With these we will feel secure. Now it is much easier to be successful. It is better to be happily achieving than trying to achieve absolute happiness.

In some ways we have invented a new game. It is a game where we have a real chance of winning all the time. We have changed the rules, but we have not cheated!

Look at this chart of what we have done.

VALUE	OLD RULE	NEW RULE
Security	Mortgage paid off	Any mortgage reduction
	Liked by everyone	Being an effective friend
	Job safe	Learning new skill
	Lifelong partnership	Developing relationships

Exercise 3   Values and Rules

Draw up some boxes for yourself with your own core values and do the same exercise. The importance of the exercise is to train yourself to draft rules which are going to empower you to meet them and thus keep your values alive. Very few of us have ever really considered the design of our own rules which is why we do not always feel the experiences we hope for.

People often make life difficult for themselves when their rules for success are centred round *'I am successful when I am the best'* or *'I am a failure if anyone does better than I do.'* In the first situation you will seldom feel yourself a winner; the second will make success in your own eyes a very distant prospect.

See what happens if those rules are changed to *'I succeed every time I take action towards my goal or any time I learn something'* and *'I only fail if I give up or if I refuse to learn.'* Suddenly we are in a win/win situation with ourselves. Feeling successful in itself leads to success.

Some people brought up in the *'**No pain, no gain!**'* tradition may feel this is a soft option which may lead to a lack of drive.

Do not follow that line.

Keep your goals high but do not make your rules for feeling good dependent on reaching them. Feeling good on the journey will take you towards and past your goals in any case.

Create rules that empower you. If your rule is *'I feel successful when I am loved,'* then you are dependent on other people and their actions and attitudes. Change it to *'I feel successful when I love someone'* and you have retained control.

You need to make sure that your rules are not designed in such a way that they create barriers with other people. People often make things unintentionally difficult for each other by being unaware that their rules conflict.

If my rule says *'We should talk things through'* and your rule says *'We should put things behind us'*, we could be heading for trouble. If my rule for respecting others is to leave the room during a conflict, and your way of showing **dis**respect is the same, we could both be heading for disaster if we happen to disagree!

Rules should be realistic.

A man was heard to say *'I don't ask for much in a woman. She just has to be tall, rich, beautiful, smart, funny, honest, sexy, helpful, patient, kind and independent.'* - Some Rule!

It takes some energy and honesty to create new rules. The reward is that setting them up and following them will enable you to experience your values more continuously. That will keep you motivated as you move towards your goals in line with your compelling vision.

L E A D E R S H I P

Because it links the subjects of 'Values' and 'Leadership' the last paragraph of the last chapter is worth repeating.

It takes some energy and honesty to create new rules. The reward is that setting them up and following them will enable you to experience your values more continuously. That will keep you motivated as you move towards your goals in line with your compelling vision.

That, of course, is the most important alignment. Start and finish with that vision. As you begin the journey towards it you should realise that it will involve management and leadership. They are both important, each in its own way, but you need to be aware of the essential difference between them. Stephen Covey in his book *'The Seven Habits of Highly Successful People'* puts it this way:

- *Management* is doing things right.
  Leadership is doing the right things.

- *Management* is the skill which builds the ladder.
  Leadership is leaning the ladder against the right wall.

- *Management* makes sure that we have the equipment. to clear a path through the jungle. **Leadership** makes sure that we move through the jungle in the right direction.

Leadership takes the premier position because it corresponds to what can be called the first creation. Everything is created twice, first in the mind and second in the physical world.

To create a house, the architect must first design it in his mind. Then he will be able to draw up the plans for the builder as he translates the idea through the plans into reality. To make sure that this is properly done he must continually check the developing building against the original vision.

In the same way, in your own life, it is your power of personal Leadership that creates the vision and design for your future. It is your Management, your executive skills, that brings that future into reality.

Vision and leadership come first.

Without the vision there is no first creation and there can be no second creation. Everything follows from the vision. The vision of leadership creates our values, decides our goals and also provides the beliefs and the motivation necessary to reach them.

Sometimes the link between the first creation in the mind and the second in the physical world can be easily understood as in the case of the architect and the house. However even in straight-forward situations we must be ready to exercise flexibility. We need to be aware of the fact that we are acting now - in the present moment - and that the present moment can be unpredictable.

We are all in that situation all the time. That is the way life works. We are living at the leading edge of our own lives.

Here the future becomes the present. Here and now is the most exciting place in the world to be. This is where the action is. So what a mistake it would be if we think of the unexpected changes that will inevitably arise from life's unpredictability as threats or as problems indicating failure.

If we have been brought up in a negative, inhibited world, that will be how we have been taught to see things. We will be in a state of constant insecurity which makes us interpret a lack of instant success as a failure. It gives us an excuse to give up.

'*I always knew it wouldn't work*' is the standard cop-out for the negative thinker who transfers blame away from himself.

When the second creation fails to follow automatically from the first, people find it easy, as they get upset, to blame others and to write the project off. This is a pity. It involves such great waste. Thomas Edison put it like this:

'*Many of life's failures are people who did not realise how close they were to success when they gave up.*'

Edison was in a position to make that judgement. When he had the first creation (or invention) of the light bulb, he had made almost two thousand unsuccessful attempts at the second creation to make a light bulb that would work. He was asked if he was happy with the idea of heading towards yet another failure. Edison replied that he had not failed at all, he had simply succeeded in identifying almost two thousand ways not to do it.

The next experiment produced the working light bulb!

In a similar way, many of the people who achieved great success did so in spite of the voices of discouragement. They insisted on staying on the leading edge.

After Fred Astaire's first screen test, the memo from the testing director of MGM in 1933 said *'Can't act! Slightly bald! Can dance a little!'* Astaire kept that memo framed over the fireplace in his Beverley Hills home.

The Beatles were rejected by the Decca label because someone said *'There is no future for groups with a line-up of three guitars and drums.'*

Socrates argued that virtue is knowledge, vice is ignorance and that no one wittingly does wrong. He was sentenced to death on charges of atheism and of corrupting the minds of the young.

One expert critic said of Vince Lombardi, *'He possesses minimal football knowledge. Lacks motivation.'*

Beethoven handled the violin awkwardly and played his own compositions to improve his techniques. His teacher called him hopeless as a composer.

Enrico Caruso's parents wanted him to be an engineer. His teacher said he had no voice and could not sing.

Albert Einstein did not speak until he was four years old and did not read until he was seven. His teacher described him as *'mentally slow . . . . adrift forever in his foolish dreams.'*

When Peter J Daniel was at junior school, his teacher Mrs Phillips constantly said *'Peter J Daniel, you're no good. You're a bad apple and you're never going to amount to anything.'*

Peter was illiterate until he was twenty-six. Then a friend stayed up with him all night and read him a copy of the great inspirational book 'Think and Grow Rich'. Today, Peter Daniel owns the street corners where he used to fight and he has published a book with the title 'Mrs Phillips, You were Wrong!'

As you read those stories you realise two things.

First, it will probably strike you that teachers carry a fearsome responsibility. If you are yourself a teacher, bear that in mind. The second evident point is that all these people, like Edison, heard a louder voice than the negative voices of the other people around them. They heard the voice of their own vision. They had all become masters of the art of personal leadership. They knew how to take a positive reading out of whatever life presented to them.

All these Peak Performers had another characteristic in common. In their subsequent careers they interpreted every apparently unsuccessful attempt as a learning experience rather than as a failure.

Look at these letters: **opportunityisnowhere**

What did you read? - 'Opportunity is nowhere'? Or, like the people we have been talking about, did you come up with **'Opportunity is now here'**? - It is, as long as you view life from a positive perspective.

> Two shoe salesmen were sent out to Africa. They both sent telegrams back to headquarters. The first read *'There is no market out here. No one wears shoes'*. The second one read *'No one here wearing shoes. Send 5 million pairs as soon as possible.'*

Do you have any doubt which was the more successful?

Not all goals are the result of a series of logical moves from first to second creation as happened with Edison and the light bulb. After all, if second creation followed automatically from the first, what would this mean? There would be no need to learn anything. There would be no growth. If there were not adventures between conceiving and achieving a goal, would there be any value in the goal? No! The journey in many ways matters more than the arrival.

Sometimes the journey opens up new creative possibilities. As we move forward we meet feedback which can either give us a feeling of insecurity or we can experience it in a positive way. The solution is always in the problem. Even though they first appear to **ob**struct us, obstacles come to **in**struct us.

Every obstacle is in truth an opportunity. To the positive thinker and the Peak Performer problems exist to generate solutions.

In turn, each solution creates a new bigger space into which we can move forward. Looked at in this light, 'problems' should be re-christened 'challenges'.

When challenges are handled from this perspective our behaviour changes so much that we are more than likely to overshoot our original target. Columbus did not set off to discover America, but he did learn the way there en route to what he originally believed was his destination!

Whether our goals are precisely defined in advance or whether they are discovered through opportunities found on the journey, the more goals we reach, the more we will be able to reach.

Like explorers, every time we reach the horizon a new landscape opens before us and new possibilities are on offer. However the purpose of the exercise does not lie in arriving at some final destination. It lies in who and what we become as we make the journey.

Once you accept this, you move into a new dimension. This is the final proof of the superiority of positive over negative thinking. That is not just a meaningless claim; it is entirely in line with the truth. In science, a theory is held to be true when it resolves more issues than other theories. The best systems are those yielding the richest harvests. Our model of the multiplication and expansion of goals is a case in point.

The contrasting model of negative thinking, which always sees every challenge as a reason, an excuse or even an opportunity for giving up, just cannot compete. Positive thinking, the philosophy of Peak Performers is just too good to be untrue!

Arthur L Costa, Professor of Education at California State University, said *'The best way to predict the future is to invent it now.'* To do so, we must learn to make our inventions co-operate with reality. For hundreds of years we have been trying to dominate nature yet look at the ecological mess we have created. We must learn a more intelligent way forward.

Our pursuit of self-development as an end in itself as we seek to unfold our potential allows us to value **serendipity**. This *'faculty of making happy chance finds'* becomes increasingly more relevant as we move along the path. It leads to a greater wisdom than that of trying to establish absolute control within rigid parameters. We can trust the world to give us its best if we give it our best.

Our relationship to reality is not very different from our relationship to other people. You aim for a goal. You plan your route. However, you do not have to stick rigidly to every planned step. There are likely to be moments when it is wise to relax and let the world come to you. *'You do not need to push the river; it flows all by itself.'*

In the last chapter we talked of **Values**. For all of us, both as individuals and as a species, our highest value is to fulfil our potential. Of course we have other values, many of which are subsidiary goals. They may be money, family or possessions. They are symbols of our values in that they represent something we may want to feel. That may be power, love or security. Do not mistake **means** values for **ends** values.

You may find the new BMW or that sought-after promotion brings instant happiness. However that pleasure may well be transitory, particularly if it is followed by uncertainty about what to do next. Perhaps you have forgotten that each material goal is only a symbol for a step towards the next greater goal and your own true value.

We all know stories of people who were apparently successful as they achieved many remarkable goals but who ultimately and tragically failed because they never achieved their values. Think of Elvis Presley or Marilyn Monroe. You may have your own examples. One thing which they all underline is the importance of always establishing a new goal on a new horizon line.

We must keep moving forward and developing. Constant self-development is an end in itself and each goal is a device to activate that development. Now that we know what goals are for and now that we have rules that work **for** us rather than **against** us we can line up many of the usual obstacles and demolish them.

- Fear of failure
- Poor self-image
- Pre-conditioned attitudes
- Creation of excuses

Remember if we are not moving forwards, we are more than likely falling backwards. A man who is going nowhere will always be sure that that is exactly where he will arrive.

Leadership is what this is all about, particularly leadership of yourself. People talk of being **pro**-active or **re**-active. Peak Performers will always stand on the proactive side of that dividing line.

Reactive people wait for things to happen. Their language absolves them of responsibility. They love excuses. They have a list as long as you like.

    ✶ It's the lack of resources.   ✶ It's the management.
    ✶ It's the competition.   ✶ It's the location.
    ✶ It's the lack of competition.   ✶ It's the recession.
    ✶ It's the weather.   ✶ It's the government.
    ✶ It's the lack of teamwork   ✶ It's the staff
    ✶ It's the customers.   ✶ It's the social system.
    ✶ It's the product.   ✶ It's the suppliers.
    ✶ It's my family background   ✶ It's my other half.

Perhaps, not remarkably, '*It's never **me**'*. Yet it is only when we take leadership responsibility for our own life that we begin to acquire the power to change the situation for the better.

B L A M E   O R   A I M

The following statements were made in writing to an insurance company in support of drivers' claims following various accidents:

'The other car collided with mine without giving warning of its intentions.'

'I collided with a stationary lorry coming the other way.'

'A pedestrian hit me and went under my car.'

'The pedestrian had no idea which way to run, so I had to run over him.'

'The telephone pole was approaching. I was attempting to swerve out of its way when it struck the front end.'

These statements may all seem funny but in many ways they are sad. The people who wrote them were not amused, nor were they successful in their claims. That is not where the sadness lies. The sadness is in the negativity of the approaches. Someone or something else must be at fault. But will this transference of responsibility help? Quite simply - No!

Of course the examples above are particularly ludicrous, but they are symptoms of a serious problem. If I am having difficulty with a colleague and say '*He makes me upset*', I am handing over control of my emotional life to that other person.

How often have you heard someone say things like '*My God! This computer really annoys me!*'? What are they actually saying? Has the computer a mind of its own? The more we think in these terms of blaming other people, or even inanimate objects, the more we are handing over control of our lives.

It would be stupid to deny that there are some situations that are beyond our control. There are certainly times when the other person genuinely is at fault. In spite of that, the best strategy is to act as though we ourselves are responsible and have the power to make positive change. That way, even if we do not have control, we maintain personal power.

Take responsibility even when it is not your fault.

Which is going to have the better result - blaming the other person when things go wrong (whoever is at fault), or resolving to establish a better rapport with them?

Blaming others is not an option for Peak Performers. It never improves our performance. Blaming others is disempowering because it means handing over control. So what is the answer when something does go wrong?

If everyone concerned in a situation is in the negative mood they will all be looking for someone to blame and that will include you. Passing the buck is one of the ways everyone tries to avoid taking responsibility. If we try it ourselves and blame someone else, we are handing that other person the empowerment over the situation which includes ourselves. In a structured management we may try to pass the buck to someone senior in an attempt to justify the blaming process. *'Why should I sort out the problem? It's his responsibility.'*

In the same structure we may complain at another time about the way the same person 'above' us restricts our freedom! We cannot have it both ways. We need to realise that when we blame others we are actually giving them our permission to have that degree of authority in our lives.

Remember, a problem is merely an opportunity in a temporary disguise. It may well be an unforeseen complication in the territory between first and second creation. We should not be surprised when such complications turn up. They are part of the rich reality of the adventure of creation. As long as we have faith in the project which we are creating we will recognise the opportunities which the problems are offering. The moment we stop doing so, we find ourselves back in the badlands of seeking excuses, of trying to run away from our own challenges.

In the last chapter we listed some Peak Performers from Astaire to Einstein. They got beyond the difficulties of other people's negativism because they had an aim which was stronger than any need to blame. The aim was strong enough to see the opportunities in the complications which surrounded them.

Einstein was struck by the inconsistencies in Newtonian Physics. He had enough confidence in his own adventurous imagination not to avoid looking at this problem. For years most of his contemporaries had ignored the inconsistencies. They blamed the limitations of the mathematics which they used as they measured physical systems.

Einstein saw the opportunity and asked the questions which led to his Theory of Relativity on which so much of modern physics is based. It is exciting to hear that people today are ready in turn, to challenge Einstein's revolutionary thinking. Latest advances in mathematical thinking have taken the horizons of their vision steps further as they believe they have come up against 'problems'. They see those inconsistencies as challenges demanding Peak Performance from them.

What do most people do when they are in a 'blame' mentality? To be more specific and more blunt, what do **we** do in that situation? We label a complication as a problem. Then we start to steer ourselves downhill with a series of negative questions.

What is the *problem*?
How long have I had this *problem*?
Whose fault is it?

Why did the *problem* arise in the first place?
Why haven't *they* done anything about it?
Why haven't *they* solved it?

Each question takes the acceptance of the existence of a problem one stage further. The possibility of a solution fades further away. You can hear the air leaking out of the balloon! We have experienced failure.

What happens if we replace the 'blame' mentality with an 'aim' mentality?

To begin with we see the situation as a challenge and we look for desired outcomes. New questions are put.

How will we know when we have *achieved* this outcome?
Who can *help* us?
What can I *contribute to* the achievement?
What resources would be most *useful*?
What can I *learn* from this?

As we ask these questions, a sense of possibility surrounds us. We will expect and experience positive feedback. We can feel the up-currents of air under our wings.

What has made the big difference? Like Christopher Columbus on his journey to America, we have discovered that we have embarked on a learning experience. In choosing to aim rather than to blame, we begin to reap the rewards of taking responsibility.

Being responsible is largely a matter of being '**response**-able', that is being able to respond. This is quite different from the negative concept of only being **re**-active. Being responsible means not only being ready and able to respond to a situation or a challenge but also being able to see that there are different ways of doing so. We are no longer blinkered by the philosophy of blame transference which holds us to a consistently narrow path bounded in by the concept of '*What can **I** do? It was someone else's fault.*'

This personal responsibility brings freedom and particularly the freedom to choose our response. We open up a whole range of possibilities in our lives.

We will never be aware of our potential until the day we take responsibility for our own lives. It will never become apparent at all if we allow someone else to make our decisions - or to take the blame!

The real challenge is that when we take responsibility we have to be ready to abandon our excuses for failing to get the best out of ourselves.

We are familiar with many excuses based on our circumstances or our environment. We know all about the easy way out, for example when we blame our parents or even our grandparents. Those excuses are no longer valid or available to you when you make the responsible decision to take control of the architecture of your own future.

We cannot fudge this issue or make a compromise about it. If you want to be a Peak Performer, the acceptance or avoidance of responsibility is not a matter of choice. Acceptance is mandatory. Responsibility and power are two sides of the same coin. Only the taking on of complete responsibility gives us complete power over ourselves. We either make progress or we make excuses. We can not do both.

'What the mind of man can conceive, the will of man can achieve.'

The power to do this lies within ourselves. It does not lie in our personal history. It does not lie in our society. It does not lie in our environment. It lies within ourselves.

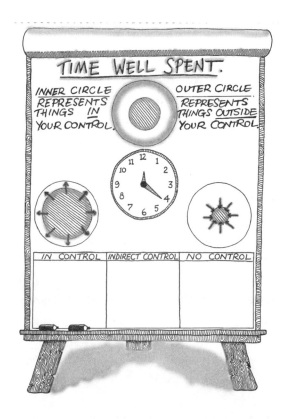

Consider this diagram. At the top you can see two concentric circles with the inner one shaded. This inner circle represents things that are within your control. Covey calls it your *Circle of Influence*. The outer circle represents things which may be important to you but over which you have no direct control. This is your *Circle of Concern*.

Think how much time many of us spend worrying about things in the outer circle. Our concerns may be worthy and well-intentioned. We surely sympathise sincerely with the victims of Third World dictatorships. We may be seriously worried about global warming. As long as we have no control over these things that concern us, our **worry** may be futile, or even worse than futile. Once again we can find ourselves disempowered by feelings of frustration as the world 'out there' is pressuring us.

Now look at the inner circle where we can focus on things which we **can** influence. If we concentrate our effort there, the more we achieve, the more we will be in a position to have effort to spare to have effective influence in what will be an increasing circle. This happens both in a gradual and in a measureable way as we expand our centre of self-empowerment.

Ancient Tibetan Buddhists used to insist that if a man was to lock himself away in a room and see no-one for the rest of his life, if that man was to think ten true thoughts, he would change the history of the world!

Shakespeare knew of the need for readiness to accept the unexplainable.

'There are more things in heaven and earth, Horatio, than are dreamed of in your philosophy.'

 Great leaders as far apart from each other as Mahatma Gandhi and Abraham Lincoln began by focusing on their circle of influence. Once they had taken responsibility for that area, their 'response-ability' grew and their impact on their much greater circles of concern became inevitable. They offer classic examples of the consequence of the 'inside-out' approach which we recommended earlier.

As we are, so our world comes to be. That is not over-statement. Here we are specifically dealing with our world in the sense of the circles in which we move and of which we are a part.

That is perhaps a rather selfish interpretation of the significance of the potential impact of change. If one man or woman changes, those around that person will change. If one family changes, their community will change. If communities change, nations change. It is a geometric progression. Taking it back to the beginning, we can underline the potential impact of what we are saying in one challenging sentence.

As I am, so is my nation.

> John Henry was the richest man in town. He owned shops, hotels, the local sawmill and the land and woods around it. Henry John was a local lumberjack who worked in the woods. John Henry indulged in all the bad habits wealth could bring and his health was poor. Henry John had very little money but was the strongest healthiest man in town.
>
> When a wizard offered each of them a wish, they both asked to change places. John wanted health and strength. Henry wanted wealth. By magic, each man's soul moved into the other's body.
>
> At first they were delighted. John Henry might now be nearly broke but he had never felt so healthy. Henry John could suddenly begin to indulge expensive tastes. Before long, however, they both became restless.

John Henry began to be fed up with his poverty and put his innate ability at money-making to work   starting up new businesses from small beginnings. Henry John soon grew tired of the flabbiness of his new body and began to take exercise in the woods. As he did so, the businesses began to slip from lack of attention and the money drained away through his expensive spendings.

As you might expect both men ended up back where they started. Once again John Henry became the town's leading businessman but he gradually began to lose his new-found health as the demands of the business world tied him more and more and growing success tempted him back to his old self-indulgent ways.

Henry John eventually found his money gone as his businesses began to collapse from neglect. However he was fit and healthy and was soon recognised as the best lumberjack in the area.

You can draw the moral of the story for yourself.

We create our own destinies. Unless we change internally we recreate the same external circumstances. The inside-out model is clearly at work. Accepting responsibility is the only way to go. Of course it is a challenge, but it brings power and freedom.

In these inside-out situations, if we are to achieve a positive and successful outcome, we must be able to resist not only our own negativity but other people's as well.

Many years ago, a man who hated the Buddha wandered the world seeking for a chance to unload all his negativity on the Enlightened One.

Eventually he got his opportunity. He was granted an audience with the great man.

He sat at his feet and let a violent tirade of abuse pour out. The Buddha listened patiently and seemed in no way put out.

Once the man had finished he was so amazed by the Buddha's lack of reaction that he had to ask him how he remained so calm.

'Well,' said the Buddha, 'If someone offers a present to another and the present is declined, to whom does that belong?'

The man thought for some time, then replied, 'To the giver, I suppose.'

'Exactly,' said the Buddha.

We must not only take responsibility, but, as we decide to be pro-active, we become immune to negativity - whether our own or other people's.

As Eleanor Roosevelt said,

'No one can make you feel inferior without your consent.'

V I S I O N -

A N   E X E R C I S E

W e have repeatedly referred to the central importance of your personal vision. It belongs at the centre of the wheel of your life.

It is not something **we** can define for you because it must be entirely yours. What we can do is help you to see it for yourself and fill in the detailed picture.

At the moment you may have a clear vision, or you may feel rather vague about it or even be unsure of what a vision consists of. Whatever your situation, that is fine.

However, you will find that the moment you start to take action towards realising your potential, your vision will begin to take shape.

Although we cannot define your vision for you, we have an exercise which will help you. It is something which we have to do together, although our part lies in supplying the script.

What we are going to outline is an exercise in '**visualisation**'.

You will get used to this idea, but, for the time being, just regard it as an unusually vivid experiment in using your imagination.

We are going to suggest a screenplay. You may wish to change it or to elaborate on it to suit your own needs. What we suggest you do is read it through until you are familiar enough with it not to need to read it from the page as you run the movie through your mind. Ideally you want to have the whole thing on tap both in pictures and in words.

This whole concept may be a new experience for you, and, as with any other new thing it is important to be able to stand on your feet before you try to walk, and to learn to walk before you try to run. For that reason we will divide the scenario into three segments. The first is to demonstrate to you that you have the ability to carry out the exercise. The second will expand your capacity and the third stage will give you the opportunity to identify potential positive changes in your personal vision for your future.

Exercise 4   'Screen Play'
Stage One

Find a comfortable lounging chair or somewhere you can really relax. Put on some gentle and relaxing music. Close your eyes and allow yourself to separate from your relaxing body. Float above yourself and look down at what you see. You can see yourself lying relaxing there, as if you were looking down from the ceiling of the room. Now come back down again and re-enter your body. Open your eyes. That completes Stage One.

That should not have been too difficult. However if you found any problems with it, stop here and try it again. You may find it helpful to imagine that you are looking at a photograph of yourself - except that you are living and breathing.

When it works, you are ready to move on to Stage Two.

Stage Two
This begins in exactly the same way as Stage One but this time, once you have floated clear, do not stop at the ceiling.

Float higher until you can see the whole house, then on until you can see the street and then the whole neighbourhood below you. Accelerate as you move higher and higher until you can see the geography of the whole area, the rivers, the mountains, eventually the coastline of the whole country and the sea around it.

On you climb and float until you begin to see the whole curvature of the planet Earth and on until eventually you have a stupendous view of the planet itself swimming like a blue sphere wrapped in clouds and itself surrounded by the dark vastness of space.

Now let everything slow down as you contemplate this place - this world - which is your home. Realise that you belong to it. Remember that person relaxing down there so many miles below. Realise that you can go back down there, taking with you the sense of perspective on life that you have now.

Take it back so that the person there will be aware of that new perspective and not allow themselves ever again to become lost in the immediate demands of life.

Now gradually begin to make your way back down again. As you come within the curve of the planet you can see seas and continents. Further down you see your country, your neighbourhood, your street, your house, your room until you are once again floating above yourself. Pause there for a moment and absorb the experience before you return to yourself. That is Stage Two.

Stage Three

When you have mastered the mental exercise of the first two stages, you can take advantage of the pause in Stage Two to use your new perspective to look at your life. Use your imagination to see your past and your future as railway lines moving towards and away from the place where you are now.

Look closely at the line from the past. On that track can be found all your experiences. Some will be pleasant experiences, some will be learning experiences. Then there are the others like a train hauling a heavy load along the line. That train is struggling in low gear burning up energy as it struggles up a steep slope. The load is the garbage of the mistakes of the past. What can the train driver do?

He can hear the strain in the engine and the shriek of the wheels as they slip on the rails. He makes a decision. He climbs down and uncouples those trucks full of trouble and disaster.

You must accept the past for what it is. Uncoupling those overloaded trucks may mean taking action to clear out the garbage with which they are filled. There will be things to be put right and dealt with. You will have no problem recognising them, as long as you are prepared to face them honestly. Once they have been sorted out you will have a new freedom.

Suddenly the train is free and the trucks get smaller and smaller as they are left in the distance. There is a sense of release and lightness and the driver enjoys the feeling as the train moves away from the track of your past, ready to move onto the track to the future.

With the freedom you have created you can follow the train

along that track to the future. The past will no longer control it. You can design it. You can change its destination. The power to do so is yours. Look all the way up the track as far into your future as you can imagine and see an image of yourself in five years, or ten, or twenty. See that image of yourself as you want to be at that time. See that self as the successful outcome of living by the values and the vision of your present self.

Connect yourself with that future self and allow the wisdom and fulfilment of that future person to flow into your present knowledge and generate confidence and awareness of what can lie ahead.

Now float back down to the present self.

Bring with you all the things you have learnt so that they become an integrated part of you. Be aware of the sense of confidence and calm certainty as you re-enter your body. Stretch and feel your limbs as your awareness returns to the here and now, where you began.

You can run this programme any time you feel the need. By learning how to detach yourself from inside and see yourself from outside, you will find yourself uniquely placed to identify where you are coming from, what may be holding up that train and what needs to be done to switch the points to the track to that positive future.

BREAKTHROUGH TO PEAK PERFORMANCE

Part Two

MASTERING YOUR MOTIVATION

THE

PERFORMANCE

SCALE

Each of us has a destiny and that destiny is unique. At the same time we all have something in common. In every case, our destiny is a matter of realising our potential. We all have the potential to be more than we are today - that is why we are alive.

Our destiny can change even though it is unique. This book is a manual for success and it assumes that the measure of our success is the measure of how much of our potential we have realised.

It is important to appreciate that success is not a matter of how well we do in comparison with others. It is how we measure up to the best in ourselves.

The quest to fulfil our potential is what brings happiness. Nothing is more useful in that quest than aiming for a goal. Notice that it is **aiming for** rather than **reaching** the goal which is critical.

Goals are there to give us purpose and direction.

Two mediaeval labourers were chipping away at blocks of stone. One was obviously full of energy and interest in his work. The other looked bored stiff.

A passer-by asked them what they were doing.

The bored man answered 'I'm chipping away at this block of stone.'

His companion smiled as he answered 'I am building a cathedral.'

If you think you can identify your full potential now, you are always going to be limited by today's thinking and your growth will steadily grind to a halt.

A whole cathedral is a distant goal. The enthusiastic carver probably had short-term goals as well, like completing so many blocks today or this week. We need to link our long-term goal to mid-range and short-term goals, because we know that the achievement of reaching each goal along the way gives us new energy to set off towards the next.

Motivation is the fuel we use in reaching our goals. We must control that fuel supply ourselves, because, if we believe other people are in charge, we will not have the free access which we need. Most of us have been conditioned to accept that we are people to whom things are done; we are people to whom things happen. Somehow the real power is 'out there.'

This outside-in model encourages a passive, unadventurous and reactive stance towards life. Throughout history it has been actively encouraged by those in authority. Automatically obedient people are easier to control. But as we have already underlined, the passive/re-active model will get you nowhere. Is that your target?

The fuel supply leads back to the individual as its source. Every major change in history, every great movement in art, every important advance in science can be traced back to one person.

If we feel that our lives are shaped by forces beyond our control, think again of the words of Eleanor Roosevelt which we quoted earlier, '**No one can make you feel inferior without your consent.**'

Our belief about this is critical to the state in which we live. We are going to use that word '***State***' as a core part of our thinking. Here it means the psychological condition, not the external situation. It means mood, but much more. It indicates our overall temperament and disposition. It includes our attitude to everything around us.

We are going to measure **State** on a performance scale of 1 to 10. Where we are on that scale depends on the attitudes we have built up over time. As our attitude changes positively, we move up the performance scale. This is not because we have had a sudden improvement in our ability. It is because we have learned how to access the abilities we already have, and how to use them to our best advantage.

What kind of State results if we believe ourselves to be dominated by outside forces and if we are prepared to accept that situation? It is exemplified by the lives of the institutionalised. It is the state of disempowerment.

If the State we are in were measured in terms of resourcefulness on that scale of 1 to 10, those who allow themselves to be so disempowered are on a permanent measure of 1. What is more, their condition becomes constantly repeating and takes on all the power of a self-fulfilling prophecy.

For most of us, things are not that bad. We fluctuate. Sometimes we feel and act as though we are free agents. At other times we may feel and act as though everything is being determined for us. This is because we have no clear idea of where we stand and what we believe. It is part of the old philosophical debate between freewill and determinism.

We like to take the credit when things are going well, but, very quickly, when things begin to go wrong, we look for someone to blame, so that we can claim that the situation was not under our control.

That will not do. The time has come to decide. It was a Zen Master who said to one of his students *'Either sit straight or fall over! Just don't wobble!'*

We have enough information to know that we have the power within ourselves to decide our own outcomes. We have enough experience to understand that if we want the power we have to accept the responsibility.

You are going to have to accept that responsibility for yourself. If you are not prepared to do so you may as well stop reading this book here and now!

Try this experiment.

Exercise 5   'The Citric Mini-Movie'
Cup your hand and imagine there is a big juicy lemon in it. Now, lift the lemon, bite into it and taste the juice. Close your eyes and really imagine the whole sensation.

What happened?

The chances are that your mouth began to fill with saliva, just as though you had been sucking on a real lemon.

What does that prove?

It proves that your nervous system often can not tell the difference between a real and a vividly imagined event.

A famous hypnotist begins each day by imagining himself on holiday. For half an hour he relaxes, imagining himself lying on the beach of an island in the sun, listening to the waves gently lapping on the shore.

Imagine how relaxed and refreshed he feels at the start of his day! Would you like to start your day feeling that way?

Perhaps you may want to dismiss that as facile and superficial. Perhaps you see it as 'merely' imaginary. If that is the case, we believe that it is time for you to revise your estimate of just how powerfully imagination can affect reality.

Reality may be all kinds of things. In fact it **is** all kinds of things. However one thing is certain. Whatever else it may be, reality can only be what we experience. For each of us the whole of reality is the sum of our experiences. That is true for everyone.

Experience is largely a question of where we choose to focus.

If you have ever been driving a car that has gone into a skid, you will remember the terrible fixation on what you are convinced you are going to hit. Racing rally drivers learn a very useful different skill. They force themselves to concentrate on the direction they want to **go**. The result usually is that that is where they end up.

We always move in the direction of our attention both literally and figuratively in the case of our psychological expectations and pre-suppositions. Remember the circles of influence and concern. They underlined the importance of focus.

Peak Performers learn to focus away from the problem and towards the solution.

Lottery winners who do not quickly become **mentally** rich, but who maintain their 'poor person' mentalities, will soon find ways to lose all the money they have won. If you go through life afraid of falling over, guess what is likely to happen!

We need to be clear here. We are not saying that we can ignore what is going on all around us and rely entirely on living inside the world of our imagination. Disempowered people who feel trapped at their low point on the performance scale often try to do just that. They achieve correspondingly poor results.

What we are suggesting is that the internal and external aspects of our lives form a loop in such a way that our State and our Results constantly re-inforce each other.

Consider this model of motivation.

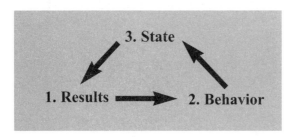

Many of us go through life using this pattern. We believe that the **Results** we are getting in our lives, in other words our present circumstances, dictate our **Behaviour** which in turn conditions our **State**, or how we feel.

This is the outside-in model. It is not helpful because clearly our State will, in turn, dictate our Results. From a poor starting point we will be caught in a downward spiral.

Now see what happens if we reverse the process. Make use of the fact that we can have the power to determine our State and start from there. Reverse all the arrows.

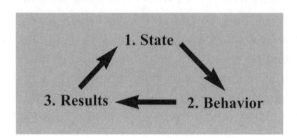

Now we have an inside-out model. A State, high on the performance scale, improves our Behaviour which in turn improves our Results. No one doubts that better Results will in turn improve our State. This is an upward spiral towards increasing success. This is the self-motivational model which empowers us. Of course it depends on starting as high as we can on the Performance Scale and that is our next objective.

C O M E   D A N C I N G

There are various strategies for hitting 10 on the Performance Scale. We have already seen that we can begin by looking problems in the face and recognising them as challenges to be welcomed.

We have seen that what might appear at first sight to be failures can be turned to advantage when they are recognised as learning opportunities.

The key is to start moving towards your goal and to keep moving, even when you have to make adjustments in the light of what you learn as you go forwards. That may sound simple, but in essence it is the fundamental secret of success borne out in the examples of the lives of Peak Performers past and present.

!

Using this pattern of behaviour, we either win or we learn. We cannot lose. Failure does not exist in this model. **Failure has been replaced by feedback.** Now, does this mean that when we set out to achieve something, our behaviour will never take us in the wrong direction? Of course not.

The first step is to know your desired outcome, your long term goal. The second step is to take action, to start moving towards the goal. To do that, you have to engage in the kind of behaviour which you believe will take you in the right direction. Now the vital third step is to notice what is working and what is not.

If something is not working, what is the next logical step? It is **change**. There is no need to be stubborn! The fourth step is totally logical. Change your approach. Change until you get it right and are once more moving in the right direction.

Remember Thomas Edison. The reason for his success was that he learnt something from every attempt. He regarded the learning as feedback and he knew that he had to try something different the next time. He kept himself high on the Performance Scale. He maintained the flexibility which is an essential and crucial Peak Performer's skill.

When an aeroplane flies round the world it only spends a comparatively low percentage of its time exactly on course, in a straight line. The navigation system constantly compensates for changes in wind currents. The same thing happens with ships at sea. Flexibility in adjusting to changing circumstances means that, although they may not always be pointing exactly at their target, both plane and ship reach their destination in the most efficient way.

Think of dancing. We call this behaviour the **DANCE**.

D   have a **D**esired outcome. Have a goal.
A   **A**ction. Take some.
N   **N**otice the results as you go.
C   **C**hange when necessary. Be ready to be flexible.
E   **E**xcellence. Aim for it. Learn from your own and other people's experience.

We must not confuse flexibility with weakness. We must not resist change because we associate it with failure.

Fortunately for us, our parents did not see us this way!

If you were asked to assist in the development of a feeble-looking creature which appeared unable to understand a word you said, which could not talk, which could not control its bodily functions, which could not even walk, how much of your energy and time would you be prepared to spend on its development? Fortunately, all of you who are or will be parents are willing to dedicate enormous amounts of both time and energy to the future of the human child which we have just described!

When the child falls over we do not say *'Right. That's it. You blew it! No more walking for you.'* We do not label the child as a failure.

We know that the baby will learn from the experience and become more and more proficient every time it climbs back onto its feet. Our faith in it is not misplaced.

Within a few months the child will have learned to walk and will have also learned the basics of language. It will have put together a complex space/time continuum and will have mastered a number of sophisticated social skills. Children in general are capable of the most astonishing learning feats which we generally take for granted. Much of this comes from our constructive, positive support.

Glen Dornan, author of 'Teach Your Baby To Read' estimates that *'Every child at birth has a greater potential intelligence than Leonardo da Vinci'*. From what we can see for ourselves, at that stage they are the ultimate Peak Performers.

It is a sad reflection on our society that, once we really begin on the process of social indoctrination of our children, it becomes very apparent that we are particularly good at teaching them how to become losers! In those early days our outside-in pattern of training works because the child is locked firmly into its own inside-out attitude to learning. It is when we move on to imposing our rules, often inherited attitudes and often unexplained, that the problems begin.

In the light of what we do to so many of our children, we might well be provoked into asking *'Why do we condition ourselves for failure?'* It is a fascinating question and there are two ways we can react to it.

We can spend years trying to work out the answer or we can take the short-cut and change our conditioning.

If you wake up in the middle of the night and find the house in flames, what are you going to do? Are you going to wonder how the fire started or are you going to get out of the house?

Far too many modern therapies spend their time analysing the source of the flames. Peak Performers take the nearest exit and then determine to learn some fire-fighting skills.

Implementing the self-motivation model and learning how to **DANCE** with the 'win or learn' attitude are just such skills. From this perspective, apparent failure is just feed-back which we have interpreted in a negative way. The truth is that we can learn from it whatever we need to unlock our potential.

Try learning how to juggle. There is only one way and that involves dropping a lot of balls - that's why they are called 'thuds'. In fact dropping balls is the only way to learn. What you have to realise is that dropping balls is not a failure to juggle properly, it is the only way to learn **how** to become proficient.

Imagine how you could benefit if you look at everything in your life from that perspective. For one thing you would not be afraid to take action because you would no longer see **failure** as a possible outcome of any challenge. Of course we cannot always control what happens to us on the outside. What we **can** do is choose our response to it on the inside. We may not be able to control the wind but we can learn to set a better sail!

All these ideas can be tied back to how we respond to situations when we are starting from different levels on the Performance Scale. Does it make a difference if we are feeling brilliant or when we are feeling not so good? Does our ability change when we are at 10? The answer may surprise you. Yet, when you think about it, you are the same person with the same physical and mental attributes. So how could your ability change, because the surprising answer to that last question is - *No*!

 Of course there is a difference when you approach a challenge from a 10 instead of from a 1. You will know that from your own experience. What has changed is not your ability, but **your ability to use your ability!** That is the key difference.

What has changed, and it depends on our position on the Performance Scale, is our behaviour.

An obvious consequence of these ideas is that, when you meet any challenge, whether it be making a presentation, meeting a long-lost friend, phoning a new customer or whatever, it makes sense to meet it from a 10. If excellence shows up **at** a 10, it makes sense to take action **from** a 10.

To understand how you can adjust your position on the Performance Scale it is time to introduce you to a new formula.

$$E + R = O$$

'**E**' is our Experience - what is happening to us at the moment.

'**R**' is our Response - how we deal with what is happening.

'**O**' is the Outcome - which is determined by our Response to the Experience.

Everyone in a given situation is faced with the same 'E' but not everyone decides to make the same Response. Hence the many different outcomes.

> Tom was a drunken bully who made a mess of his life. He had two sons Dick and Harry. Dick was a drunken bully and made a mess of his life. Harry was loving and caring and became brilliantly successful. When they were asked how it was that their lives turned out the way they did, both Dick and Harry said the same thing.

'What do you expect with a father like mine?'

Obviously they both started from the same experience. It was not what happened to them that made the difference, but how each of them chose to **respond** to that experience.

We have already seen that the best way to build up a system of powerful response is twofold. Firstly we need to throw out unproductive ideas about failure. Secondly we need to look for positive meanings from our experiences. Both of these enable us to improve the quality of our response which is the key that controls everything else.

Exercise 6   'Response - abilities'

Where do you stand at the moment? Look at this next chart and then follow the instructions.

EXPERIENCE	YOUR RESPONSE	YOUR RESULT (1-10)
PROBLEM		
FAILURE		
REJECTION		

At the moment how do you respond to a problem? Do you attack it at once? Do you put off dealing with it? Do you try to pass it on to someone else? Try to be honest and fill in your answer. Then mark yourself out of 10 on the Performance Scale in the Result column. Ask yourself similar questions about your responses to each of these experiences. Once again, give yourself a mark for your result.

If you realise the significance of **E + R = O,** you may well want to improve the quality of that response column.

What have we learnt so far?

We have seen that one thing which prevents us from always being at our best is the belief that it is outside forces rather than ourselves which control us. This can lead to fatal hesitation.

We often know that we ought to do more, but the **fear of failure** makes us avoid taking action. For many of us it is this fear of failure, rather than any actual failure we have experienced which has the greater influence.

We have too many 'shoulds' in our lives, such as '*I should be able to achieve more, to sell more, to produce more*' or '*I should take more exercise.*' '*I should*' is like a line drawn only in the sand. Even a modest passing wind will shift it. '*I must*' is a line set in cement. Make the decision to turn your 'shoulds' into 'musts'. The old proverb is right. The road to hell is paved with good intentions!

Make the decision to commit to excellence. That is the key. Start to take ownership of your own life. You have the power to govern your own State. The key is State management: the ability to stay at 10, the ability to stay resourceful which comes from your commitment to excellence.

How do we do this, particularly when things may appear not to be going well?

There are several answers or skills which we can practise in response to this question. First we must be clear in our understanding of the situation which we face. Remember, to be high on the Performance Scale does not suddenly demand new abilities. It does mean allowing ourselves to **access** the abilities we already have. Remember the self-motivation model.

If we begin from our State which drives our Behaviour which in turn decides our Results, then what decides our State?

Two things:- **Focus** and **Physiology**. Focus is the way we represent things in our minds. Physiology is the way we use our bodies.

Think about Focus.

We already know our experience defines the reality which we inhabit. We need to take a step further. Our lives are a mirror image of our most consistent thoughts and expectations. So we need to target our thoughts to take us towards **who** we want to be and **where** we want to be. How and why might this work?

We know the world only in terms of the representations we make of it in our minds. We can only know our own experiences but fortunately the potential range of our experience is vast. We have access to an enormous fund of knowledge and it is recorded in our minds. When we think of the world, we do so using our experience. If the world is the **territory** our representations are our **maps.**

Human beings can create complex maps. Most other species hardly construct maps at all. By and large, animals simply react to stimuli, living entirely in the present. That has some advantages, but it makes it impossible for them to stand aside from the phenomena surrounding them and make individual decisions about them. On the other hand, because their maps are so complex, human beings can do just this. However no map is as complex as the territory itself.

The human nervous system receives thousands of signals every second, but we are able to use an elegant liaison between our five senses and our brains to prioritise them. First we ensure physical survival - we leave the burning house. Then we decide which of the other signals are most significant for us. Mental representations are the result. Our consciousness creates a virtual reality for each of us.

That is what we are calling our **map**.

It may be virtual reality but it is an astonishing affair. It is a stereoscopic, technicolour, stereophonic hologram. It is imbued with all the somatic richness which our five senses can supply. It has features so swift and sophisticated that the fast forward, rewind and editing facilities of our most advanced technical facilities look like pale imitations in comparison.

It is amazing! Our mental representations are the product of a brain that has a trillion cells. One hundred billion are active nerve cells; the other nine hundred billion glue, nourish and insulate them. Your brain can grow up to twenty thousand branches on each of those active cells. It runs a telephone exchange shuttling millions of messages between right and left. It controls a transmission system that flashes messages instantly to every part of your body. To equal just its mechanical capabilities, a computer would need to be the size of two high-rise buildings. What is more, neurologists tell us that we have so far exploited only about one tenth of the capacity of our amazing brains.

During the second Millenium we have progressed from building cathedrals to constructing spaceships that allow man to walk on the Moon. We have done this without even tapping into the greater percentage of the capacity! What do you think is going to happen when we learn how to unlock the rest of the potential of this stunning organism?

One thing is certain. The moment when we dare to begin to imagine the possibilities is the exact moment when they will start to happen. We quoted it earlier, we quote it again now.

'What the mind of man can conceive, the will of man can achieve.'

GOING TO THE MOVIES

The brain can create the dazzling brilliance of a virtual world, but it can be so convincing that some of us find it hard to distinguish it from reality. Yet it is vitally important that we should remember that it is 'only a film'. A film which our brain has created is one which we must learn how to control.

We live so much in terms of representational, symbolic systems that we are not always aware that they even exist.

> Picasso was accosted by a man who asked rather belligerently:
>
> 'Why don't you paint people the way they really are?'
>
> 'I'm sorry,' replied Picasso, 'I really have no idea what you mean!'
>
> The man pulled a photograph from his pocket and thrust it under the great painter's nose. 'Look' he said 'This is a photograph of my wife. That is how she really looks!'

Picasso looked at the photo for a few seconds. 'So your wife is really like that is she?'

'You bet she is' replied the man.

'Well,' said Picasso 'she's extremely small isn't she, and very flat!'

Picasso was never fooled by any representations, including his own. We must have the same attitude. This is particularly important when you realise that we are dealing with the maps or *movies* of the world which we are going to use to guide us through the territory.

Most of the films created by the human cultures in which we have grown up have received imprints including all the distortions, deletions and generalisations created and inherited by the group in which we live. Most of us create our own films using much the same criteria. Those films govern our expectations and colour our perceptions. They condition our

State. Therefore they have an impact on our Behaviour. Since this is happening to everyone, we impose our films on others in the same way as we find ourselves playing bit parts in theirs! The good news is that we can do something about all this. We created the films so we can change them. The map is not the territory. Maps can be altered.

Return to the film show. When we do not distinguish it from reality, we allow ourselves to be pushed and pulled in a mechanical way according to whom we have allowed to sit in the Director's chair for the time being. We must be particularly wary of finding ourselves playing in repeats. We all know of people who have suffered from abuse or trauma of some kind in early childhood and who seem condemned to replay those events for a lifetime.

The past does not have to equal the future. Peak Performers need to be ready to take action and to become the conscious Directors of their own film shows. When we look at things from that chair, we realise at once the importance of sound and vision - what we see and what we say to ourselves. As with television, we have other controls as well. We can adjust volume, brightness, colour and so on. Now we can set about enhancing those films which empower us, and reconstructing those which hold us back.

You created a short film a while back. It was 'Eating A Lemon.' It may not win any Oscars but it shows us just how to begin with simple exercises. Basic exercises can bring about effective changes.

In the Foreword to this book we warned you that we were looking for an inter-active readership. As you do these exercises, like the earlier ones in previous chapters, you may have to put the book down, try them out and return to the book for reference from time to time. That is fine. It is exactly what we hope for and what you need.

You may be used to a more passive form of reading. If you spend your time at that, you will be part of someone else's film! The keynote for Peak Performers is to take action and this book is a machine to think and act with. Reading the text is like going to a restaurant and reading the menu. If you really want to enjoy the meal and benefit from it, you have to follow the exercises.

Exercise 7   Be your own Director

Check out what we have just suggested. Get comfortable, then close your eyes and have a 'look' around. Before you know it you will find yourself in the middle of a 'film'. It is quite likely to be one you have seen before. It is amazing but it is true. There will be a picture there, ready and waiting.

Now, if you have stopped reading and done that exercise before you read this sentence, our bet is that you were captured by the show, you followed the action and you may even have forgotten why you were watching it. If you did not stop to do the exercise, do so now. Without the experience it will not be easy to follow along with us.

In order to begin to take control of the pictures we need to slow things down. We are going to direct our films by using the technique of **Memory Management**.

We constantly replay our memories and they constantly regenerate the same feelings. This is particularly unhelpful with bad memories which drag us into an unresourceful State which can limit our future action.

What would be useful would be to have some way of changing the process. We can do it by changing the way we picture that memory in our mental film show. It is important not to be afraid of resurrecting the bad memory to start with, otherwise we cannot work on it.

For example, you might select a memory of a time when you were rejected by someone or from some position you really wanted. Those are exactly the kind of intense memories that get replayed time after time.

Exercise 8   Be your own Projectionist

Now follow this exercise, dealing with that bad memory.

1. Take control.
2. Reduce the picture from cinemascope to television size.
3. Make it smaller. See it on a portable set.
4. Take the colour out so that it is reduced to black and white.
5. Turn the volume down until you can hardly hear it.
6. Defocus the picture and as you do this, push the picture further away until it is hard to recognize.
7. Just to make sure that you have mastered the process, do it all over again.

You may find, as you practise this Memory Management, that the negative images become harder to recall. You have taken control and they no longer have the same influence on your State. It is back in your own hands and that will give you better control of your future.

Remember to practise. Memory Management improves with care and attention. No skill is likely to be perfect straight away.

Exercise 9   Be your own Producer

That exercise is one of many designed to help us move up on our Performance Scale. Sometimes we need something that works more quickly. Suppose that you are at a point on the Scale lower than the 10 you need. As you read this, there is a fair chance that you may feel that you are at such a level. Pick out that number right now.

Now think back to a really pleasurable experience, whatever it was - passing an exam, lying on a beach in the sun - whatever comes to mind. Close your eyes and re-experience the occasion. Enjoy the film, dwelling on the sights, the sounds and all the other associated feelings of delight.

Really concentrate on feeling it. See everything as you saw it then.

Make the picture bigger, brighter and bolder. Bring it closer and closer. Step into it and relive the moment.

Score how you feel now. The chances are the number will have changed and moved up the scale. By thinking, you have been able to change how you feel. The message is simple and clear. You can have control over your State if you want to, and if you know how.

Another useful technique we call **Scramble**.

Exercise 10   Join the Audience

Think of a time in your memory when a client, a boss or someone in the family bothered you to such an extent that fear or anxiety is inhibiting you from positive action with the person.

Now 'Scramble' the way you remember things. Put the person in a silly costume. Give them pink hair and a red nose. Speed up the sound track until their voice sounds like a cartoon. The menace disappears. We free ourselves from the negative feelings. Use this technique any time for individuals or situations that bother you to such an extent that it keeps you from taking action.

If you are dealing with a particularly difficult situation or with emotionally painful material, you can extend this process into a further technique called **Disassociation**.

In this case you can distance yourself from the situation in the following way. Instead of creating the film show and watching it directly, imagine it on the screen in a cinema where you are among the audience. Now watch yourself watching the film and see yourself Scrambling the picture. That will begin to release you from the negative State associated with the original. It will allow you to move into a positive State of relief, amusement and confidence. See yourself becoming free from the movie in question.

Mental Rehearsal is yet another technique which can bring success.

So far each exercise has been dealing with the past. This new technique is designed to help you manage future performance. This may be a matter of preparing for an important presentation or a speech; it may be going for an interview; it may be making a sales call; it may be having a session with your boss.

Quite often the opportunities that exist for us in such future events are clouded over by our anxiety and apprehension. If we allow them a free run, those feelings almost guarantee poor performances. Sometimes they are so strong that they even lead us to chicken out of the situation altogether. We need to realise that that means missing out on any opportunity the situation may offer. We can think of this process as running a success avoidance strategy. We need to replace it with a strategy for success. It is a matter of how we represent the future to ourselves.

Athletes in training use this technique as an essential part of their training equipment. We can do as they do and create in advance the outcomes we want. You can describe it as writing the history of the future, or dreaming the future before it arrives.

Identify the positive result that might result from the situation. Picture it and focus on it. You may need to train your brain to think this way! However, as you take the time to practise, you will begin to notice that positive outcomes are becoming a matter of habit.

Focus is not just a matter of how we picture the world to ourselves. It can usefully concentrate on how we talk to our-selves. It is a matter of internal dialogue. Success is the outcome of resourceful pictures and positive internal dialogue.

Exercise 11   Arm Wrestling
Try this next proposal with a friend.

Ask the person to hold one arm straight out in front with the fist clenched. Tell them to resist your attempt to push the arm down-wards. If the person keeps saying (preferably out loud) the words '*I feel strong and confident*', you may find it quite difficult to move the arm. Now try it again while your friend repeats over and over '*I feel tired and weak.*' You may be surprised, as your friend will be, by the difference it makes.

How does this happen? Is it the power of suggestion? Is it some kind of self-hypnosis? Of course it is! That is the power of our representational system. In this case, words are creating State.

Our internal dialogue can affect our physiology directly and therefore our results. If we feed in negative thoughts we will create negative pictures and produce negative results. If we use statements like '*I can't do that*' or '*I hope I don't mess this up,*' we create poor representations. We introduce the possibility of failure up front and our performance is likely to reflect those expectations.

It works the other way too. So the challenge is to use your internal dialogue to support the likelihood of Peak Performance.

Ask yourself questions like '*How will I feel when I reach my target?*' - notice **when**, not **if** - say to yourself '*I can just see myself doing that,*' or '*I'm really looking forward to hearing the boss's comments when I have opened this new account.*'

Assume success. Give yourself positive presumptions. Remember, it is not just the words, it is the way you say them. Information and physical expression are as important to effectiveness as is the content.

Before we move on from the question of focus, we want to underline the importance of questions in activating our thinking processes. You may have noticed them throughout much of what you have already read.

Who asks the most questions? Almost certainly it is children. We have already identified them as the ultimate Peak Performers judging by the speed of their development.

Obviously there is a connection. The more we ask questions both of ourselves and of each other, the more we learn. The more we learn, the more we grow. Finally the more we grow, the more impact we have on the world around us as we expand into our circle of concern.

Millions of people saw apples drop from trees. It took a Newton to ask '*Why?*' Similarly, if you do not question Newton, you do not get an Einstein.

The quality of the questions we ask determines the quality of the life we lead. Great Peak Performers have the kind of positive outlook that results from asking high quality questions.

George Bernard Shaw said, '*Some men see things as they are and say 'Why?' I dream of things that never were, and say 'Why not?'*'

That is a massively powerful quotation. Be prepared to use it yourself.

Limited questions get limited answers. What too often limits our questions is our limited belief about what is possible. That is one of the reasons why children develop so fast. They do not have any previously fixed ideas about what is, or is not, possible.

Of course we need to be realistic about possibilities at certain stages. We may be putting together a strategy. That is in the domain of 'management.' Even so, do not rule out imagination. We must not rule out anything from the questions we ask when we are building our individual vision. In this case we are firmly in the field of 'leadership' and we have already underlined that difference.

The ultimate question to be used in every situation is *'What can I learn from this?'* This maintains flexibility and the readiness to change - the important fourth step in the DANCE of life.

We have looked at the impact of negative questions and the power of the positive. There is one group which we should steer clear of whenever possible.

The *'**What if**?'* question is usually based on anxiety.

'What if there is a better applicant for this job than me?'

'What if my partner falls in love with someone else?'

Remembering what we have already noticed about the power of focus to bring things into existence, we should be mindful of the power of our questions.

Anthony Robbins, who is one of the greatest performers and innovators in the field of personal development, describes the question as a magic tool that allows the genie in our mind to meet our wishes.

So be careful about what you ask for. You just might get it!

M O D E L L I N G

Now we know that by focusing the mind we can have an impact on our outcomes. The mind in turn is connected to the body, and each emotional state we experience can be connected to a specific physiology. For instance, the way you are sitting right now as you read this, your facial expression, the rate of your breathing, your movement, or indeed your lack of it, is telling you how to feel right now!

Exercise 12   Slouch!
Try this simple exercise - and don't worry if you feel silly doing it. No one is looking!

Sit as you would sit if you were bored and tired. Of course you might not have to move too much for this! Anyway, go on. Sit the way you would sit if you were bored and tired, tired and bored, bored and tired.

We told you to sit the way you would sit if you were bored and tired and you knew without thinking about it just how you had to change your physiology. You had to adjust your posture, your facial expression and the way you move. Now that you have done it, you are probably already telling yourself to move again, to adjust to the way you are feeling right now, which is different from the way you were feeling just a minute ago.

Now, in the second part of the exercise, sit the way you would be sitting if you were excited and full of energy. Really excited and really energised! Look at the difference in your physiology. You did not have to think about it. It happened automatically. By the way, did you also notice how quickly you were able to move from one condition to the other. Very quickly! Ask yourself who is in control of these changes. **You are**. No one else is controlling your physiology.

Quite clearly, when you do not feel so good, you will adopt a certain physiology (we call it 'Fizzy' to go with 'Focus'!). Your physiology will be linked to that feeling. Your head will be slightly down. Your breathing will be a little bit more shallow. You will adopt certain characteristic facial expressions. When you talk you will use certain intonations. You are feeling not so good and you are telling yourself how you should appear.

How often, when you are in that condition, have you heard your husband or your wife, or a friend at the office ask sympathetically *'Are you all right?'* They can read the message of your physiology too.

Just as you will react physiologically when you feel not so good, the opposite is true. When you are full of confidence and you are a lot more positive, your posture is up, your facial expression is more alert. Everything changes.

You can prove the point through one more exercise.

Exercise 14   Smile in Adversity
You will find it impossible to feel depressed if you stand upright with your chin up and a smile on your face. You may not believe that, but try it the next time you feel distressed or emotionally upset and see what a difference it makes.

As Peak Performers we are more interested in the results of actions than in the theory because it might take a long time to explain exactly how that works. What we and you need to understand is that we know how to put ourselves into a resourceful state. Keep that in mind.

The last major influence that we can bring to bear on improving our State management is possibly the most obvious technique of all. It is the use of good example. It is usually called **Modelling**. Find someone you admire and copy them. It is connected to the fifth step in the **DANCE** model - Excellence - when it is derived from other people's experience.

In the early parts of this book we have talked of learning from our own experience and that process must not be undervalued. At the same time, however, other people's experience is a treasure trove of information. Choosing the right role models to learn from is a excellent short-cut to getting results.

The simple technique of Modelling means identifying those who are getting the kind of results we want for ourselves. Then we duplicate, or model, what it is that they do which makes them particularly effective in their achievement. They may not even be consciously aware of what it is that makes them Peak Performers, but it must have a structure and any structure can be analysed and used as a model.

Success leaves clues and successful people leave clues as to why they are successful.

People sometimes worry that modelling might lead to a lack of originality. Those worries are understandable, but they should have no basis in what actually happens, provided that the reason for the modelling is constructive.

At the height of the Renaissance, art students spent long periods copying the work of recognised masters. Even Michelangelo did not think himself above the practice. When one of his fellow students asked how long they would have to go on learning in this way, Michelangelo's reply was '*until **we** can do it as well as **they** could*.' From that base and with that attitude, we know just how great he himself went on to become.

With modern technical skills, audio recording can be converted from sounds into pictures on a computer screen. At that stage the picture can be frozen and magnified so that each particle on the graph line can be analysed. This allows seamless editing and the production of ideal results.

Exercise 15   Model Making

Analysis of behaviour for the purposes of modelling can be approached in the same way. Peak Performers set out to identify the little extra differences that separate the merely good example from the very best. They may already be at the 'good' level themselves. They want to identify the possibly minor adjustment that will take them to the top and keep them there.

Modelling is a short cut to excellence.

The person whose example you choose may well have spent years of trial and error (**learning**) to achieve the results they wanted. By studying the strategy they finally evolved, you can get the same results in a fraction of the time.

Many of the most successful people in the world are dedicated modellers. This is hardly surprising because building on the previous success of others is a major factor of development in most fields. All that many people do to succeed in business is to transplant an established idea and technique from its original environment and take it elsewhere.

The brilliant success of Japan's economy has been due to expert modelling. Their businessmen, researchers, scientists and technicians are constantly taking the extra steps into new levels of excellence starting from the levels already achieved. They have been so successful that many people realise that they in turn offer challenging and effective models themselves.

Anthony Robbins, whom we mentioned earlier, has an interesting story to tell about modelling.

Quite early in his career he told a US Army General that he could take any army training programme and do it in half the time with better results. This was not exactly a modest proposal and the pay for the job they offered him was tied to successful results.

The challenge selected by the Army was to train newly enlisted men how to fire accurately with a .45 calibre pistol. The time they usually allocated was a four-day course and, even then, only 70% of the trainees reached the qualifying standard.

Robbins studied the key beliefs shared by some of the best shooters in the world. He then contrasted those with the beliefs of people who had never shot effectively. Next he analysed the strategies of the experts including the way they used their representational systems and replicated them so that he could teach them to a first time shooter. Finally he modelled the key elements of the physiological behaviour of the top performers. Armed with all this information, Robbins designed a one-and-a-half-day course for the beginners. What were the results?

When tested after less than two days, 100% of the trainees qualified and the number who achieved the recognised 'expert' level was three times higher than previously produced by the Army's standard four-day course

Robbins taught his beginners to send the same signals to and from their brains as the experts did. He made many of them experts in less than half the usual time.

Perhaps even more remarkably, he then went back to the original top performers and taught them how to exchange their strategies. The result, just an hour later, was that one man scored higher than he had for six months and another scored more bull's-eyes than had been achieved in competition in recent memory! The Army regarded it as the biggest breakthrough in pistol shooting since World War I. Robbins was suitably rewarded.

The secret of Robbins' success is not that he is a magician. However he does produce apparently magical results. He uses meticulous analysis and thorough application of the business and technique of modelling. There is no reason why you should not benefit from the same approach and the same application.

Model yourself on the expert modeller! Identify someone's performance you admire in an area where you would like to achieve similar results. Watch carefully and identify the technique. Try to teach your body to move in the same way. Practise those movements.

Next, make an internal picture of the expert performance. Then change it to a new internal image, this time of yourself, performing the same activity. This would be like watching a movie of yourself modelling the other performer as precisely as possible. Next, step inside your movie in the way you have already learnt and experience how it would feel to perform in that way. Repeat this until you feel comfortable. Now you have the strategy prepared to allow you to perform at expert level.

Go ahead and try it out in the real world!

One of the most effective keys to modelling is to elicit their strategy from the people you have identified as your ideal examples. If you get the opportunity, never be afraid to ask them to explain their own ideas. They will seldom refuse.

To begin with, true Peak Performers will not be selfish about sharing their success. And, of course, on purely human terms, we know that imitation is the sincerest form of flattery!

It is probably more effective if you ask them to run through their own performance in their imagination, to visualise it, and to describe it to you as they do so. If they do this in an atmosphere of co-operation with you, and you feel on the same wavelength with them, you will have the benefit of discovering their strategy without having to work it out for yourself, indirectly or just by observation.

If you can get an image for yourself of their State as we have defined it earlier, you will have what Anthony Robbins describes as 'the hotline to their strategy.' This could well give you a short-cut to a short-cut! We will be looking more closely at the value of the rapport this will involve, at a later stage.

People have strategies for everything: for getting up in the morning; for overcoming depression; for boiling an egg (!); for playing chess; even for writing a book. Whatever area of performance you want to enhance, find someone who is already doing it well and find out how they do it. Then do it yourself.

In case you think this strategy is something completely new to you, just remember that you are already an expert at the skill.

Almost from the day you were born and became a sentient human being, you began to model the people around you. Sometimes, of course, we have become so good at it that we get trapped in the model and forget that it is a model. This can be unfortunate, particularly because we did not choose our first models. They were forced on us; we were born into them.

As with our mental movies, awareness is all. Once we become conscious of our modelling tendencies, we can develop the skill to select and build on empowering models.

When we were young, we played lots of games beginning with 'Let's pretend.' That is an excellent way to begin. Playing is the fastest track to learning and on to success. If you want to have power, pretend to be powerful. If you want to be rich, begin thinking like a rich person. If that sounds like magic, well, it is!

The fact is that by pretending, or acting as if something is true, you put yourself into a positive physiological condition. That creates a resourceful State with empowering mental movies. Those lead to more effective Behaviour and you know the rest. Perhaps the biggest lesson you can gain from this whole section is the realisation that you already know it, if only you knew it!

Earlier we asked you to use a technique in a situation where you feel that you *'don't know.'* We all know you *'don't know,'* but now we challenge you to ask yourself - *'If you **did know**, what would the answer be?'* You will be surprised how often you will come up with an answer when you are challenged like that.

Successful people are people who ask themselves better questions and therefore create for themselves better answers.

BREAKTHROUGH TO PEAK PERFORMANCE

Part Three

THE POWER OF BELIEF

D E S I G N E R

S Y S T E M S

It is said that when Cortez arrived off the coast of South America he encountered local fishermen standing up to their knees at the water's edge going about their everyday business. He was very surprised to find himself and his great galleons being totally ignored. In fact he was being ignored because the Indians had never seen anything like this before. They did not react to the ships because they did not 'see' them. They did not see them because there was no room in their belief system for such large ships!

This incident sums up perfectly the fact that we do not live in a world where we believe what we see but one where we see what we believe. In other words, our beliefs govern our perceptions and therefore they also govern our behaviour.

Everyone has heard the stories of people who died at the exact hour which had been predicted for them by local witch doctors. It is also well documented that patients can undergo major surgery under hypnosis and feel no pain simply because *they believe at the time* that they will not feel it.

Imagine the results we might achieve if we were able to enhance all those beliefs which help us and to dismantle those beliefs which hinder and prevent us from achieving our goals. That is exactly the area which we are going to examine in Part Three as we move from Mastering our Motivation into harnessing the Power of Belief.

So far we have learnt how to manage our State or the way we feel. That is very important. It is like learning how to control a car which has gone into a skid, how to bring it back onto the road and of course how to keep it there. Beliefs go deeper than this. Beliefs are the influences which control our State in the first place. This makes beliefs of fundamental importance to our performance.

Your "Roll" model

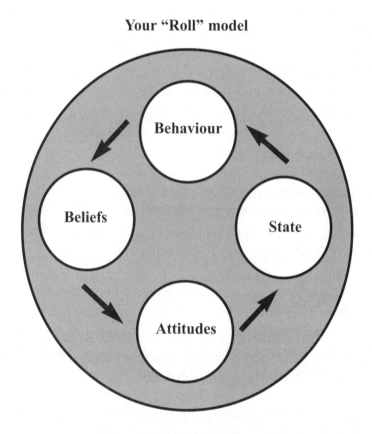

Our Behaviour is the result of our State, but our State, our feelings themselves are the results of our attitudes which in turn stem from our Beliefs. So our Beliefs are the bedrock of all our behaviour. Like an iceberg, the largest part of the structure is the part that we cannot see.

Now consider what follows.

You may believe   *'I am not a good leader.'*
        or   *'I am not confident with unfamiliar people.'*

Beliefs like those can affect whole areas of your behaviour. You may not even be aware of them because they have often become part of your sub-conscious self. Perhaps you acquired them long ago when we knew a lot less about ourselves than we know now. That would be unfortunate, since beliefs are so fundamental.

Mastering your motivation may have put you in the position of being able to change the wheel on the metaphorical car of your life, or to keep it on the road. Your belief system *designs* the vehicle and that is what you have to drive. You have to live with and by your beliefs.

It is obviously important that we should not allow ourselves to be the victims of poor design, because, once we have adopted our beliefs, it is natural that we should act as if they are true. Otherwise they would be of no value.

Our beliefs become part of our automatic response system, whether they are empowering or disempowering. So they have an over-riding impact on our behaviour.

It follows that each of us should design belief systems that work for us. We should build up those beliefs which support us and be prepared to transform those beliefs which limit us. Design your own future by taking control of your beliefs.

When you look at the 'Roll' model picture, you can see that it brings out clearly enough the part beliefs play in getting us our results. It is our belief about our potential which actually determines what actions we take and consequently the results we are likely to achieve.

Take a simple example. If a sales person believes that a certain geographical area is only capable of yielding a small amount of business, that belief will determine how much effort and action the person will take. The action in turn will lead to the kind of results that will justify and strengthen the original beliefs, thus creating and establishing a self-fulfilling prophecy.

We can connect this back to what we learnt about the self-motivation model and the significance of $\mathbf{E} + \mathbf{R} = \mathbf{O}$. Put both ideas together and you can see that we operate in terms of the following sequence:-

Stimulus ➤Response➤ State (1 to 10) ➤ Behaviour ➤Results ➤ New Stimulus - and then round again. We know that this can be either a *vicious* circle or a *virtuous* circle, depending on how we learn to control the quality of our response.

It is our response which determines our State and our consequent behaviour which will generate results that are likely to confirm our original response.

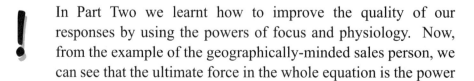

In Part Two we learnt how to improve the quality of our responses by using the powers of focus and physiology. Now, from the example of the geographically-minded sales person, we can see that the ultimate force in the whole equation is the power of belief. It is our beliefs which determine how we interpret the stimulus which gives us our response in the first place. So controlling our beliefs is yet another key.

The significance of this discovery cannot be over-emphasised. It is not enough to work at the surface level on our skills or our actions. The result will not be long lasting until we get down to the foundations.

Belief that we are able to achieve our goals has been shown by the examples of Peak Performers past and present to be a bigger factor in success than either ability or circumstances. Do not be tempted to dismiss that sentence. Not everyone can be an Einstein or a Linford Christie. Not everyone will have the goal of revolutionising scientific thought or of winning an Olympic Gold Medal. As long as anyone's goal means the fulfilment of their individual potential, achieving it is of just as great significance.

So, accept the power of belief and realise that choosing your future means designing your beliefs, because it is those beliefs which will decide whether your future happens or does not happen.

We can all be Peak Performers because individually, we each have unlimited potential. However, just how much of that potential we can really tap into depends on our beliefs, both about ourselves and about the world in general.

Therefore you need to understand how your current beliefs, whether you actively are aware of them or not, are deciding for you the amount of your potential you can access and therefore how much you can achieve.

That is because:

> ✻ The results you get in life are always linked to the actions you take.
>
> ✻ The actions you are willing to take are always in line with the beliefs that you have.
>
> ✻ Those beliefs may be inappropriate to the results you want.

Which is why you may need to **change the beliefs**.

To do that you need to understand just how it is that your beliefs are formed in the first place and how they can either inspire or prevent success.

First you need to discover how well your current belief system is supporting you. If it is letting you down, then it is time to consider how to transform the system.

What you have previously regarded as failure can be used as a step-ladder to success. Remember what you already know. There is no such thing as failure; there is only feed-back.

Next, remember that successful people are people who are willing to try something they have never tried before, and, whatever the outcome, to learn from the experience. We considered this earlier when we looked at the **DANCE** of Life model. So, have a desired outcome, take action, note the results and change where necessary.

As you follow this pattern you will begin to notice yourself using more and more of your potential. You will begin to surprise yourself! Any resistance you do meet in yourself is most likely arising from the fact that, like so many people, your beliefs run in a different direction to your desires.

Listen to a delegate who attended one of our programmes. She had a limiting belief of exactly this kind. Our conversation points up the fact that limiting beliefs are certain shortcuts to unresourceful States. This is what she said:

> *'I have had to do a lot of cold calling in the Sales Department. I'm much happier with that part of my job now, because now that you've helped me to think of rejection as a source of interesting information rather than experiencing it always as a personal failure, there's nothing hindering my motivation to pick up the phone . . . except, at the last moment, I always feel anxious and not at all inclined to get on with the job. I don't understand it really, but it's very frustrating.'*

Well, we talked it over and we decided that the problem might have something to do with her feelings about communication with other people. Quite suddenly, during our conversation, she remembered something, an early belief that she had picked up. She said:

> *'I remember having it drummed into me from a very early age that strangers could be very dangerous and that I should never talk to strangers.'*

That is a perfect illustration of a belief that was useful and valid when that lady was a child. However, it certainly is not useful to an adult who is working, cold calling in Sales! What she had to do to make things all right, was to **change** that belief.

We suggested that she had the power to choose her beliefs. In this case she needed to adopt the belief that 'strangers' could be a source of opportunity and possible benefit, rather than always existing in her mind as a threat. Once she untangled the knots in her belief system and selected this more appropriate belief, cold calling suddenly became a lot easier.

There is a point arising here which it is vital that we clarify. When we are speaking of beliefs and the need constantly to examine them to see whether or not they need to be revised, we are not challenging what people might describe as their fundamental and personal religious beliefs. Those are a matter which lies between them and their God.

What we are challenging you and everyone else to do is to examine all those other convictions by which you govern your life. These are all the things which you believe you believe, or which other people have trained you to believe, either by direct instruction or by creating the environment in which you have grown up. Those are the beliefs which need to be taken out and re-examined in the light of your present situation.

Peak Performers judge their beliefs not just as to whether they are right or wrong. They want to determine whether or not a particular belief limits or empowers them. They know that they have the power to choose. They realise that they can support or reject any belief depending on the references it relates to.

Focus on this point which we have reached. We can actually design a belief system to suit ourselves.

This idea comes as something of a shock to most people, because we are not used to thinking about beliefs as something which we can be proactive about. We tend to assume without question the belief system of the culture into which we were born. Then, like the lady in the Sales Department, we have to try to live with whatever contradictory turns and twists our inherited system imposes. We do not realise that we can do anything about our beliefs because we assume that, like the real world, they are fixed.

Yet, if we go back to what we said in the Introduction, there is nothing fixed about reality. It is conceptions which are fixed until we are flexible enough to question them. As long as we act in congruence with the world and what we can observe, reality will support us in designing an empowering belief system.

Becoming flexible in constructing, deconstructing and reconstructing our beliefs leads to a useful technique called '**Re-framing**.' All our pictures come in frames. A frame is the belief we have about something because of the perspective from which we choose to view it. For example, if you decide that now is the ideal time for a walk and it suddenly begins to rain, you might see that as ironic. On the other hand, if the garden is undergoing the worst effects of drought, rain would be a blessing.

Once the rain begins, a negative frame of mind would have us focus on the fact that we are going to have to mow the lawn, or a positive frame would see that mowing the lawn will result in a tidy garden instead of a wilderness. If we are involved in heavy work at garden maintenance, we might think of that as a waste of time and energy, or we could see it as a way of keeping fit! You can go on framing and re-framing your own pictures. You will have caught on to the idea.

Interpretations, the frames we put around everything, cascade in this same way through everything we do.

Re-framing is the practice of taking a seemingly negative situation and putting a positive frame around it.

This can involve taking a wider view, putting things in a larger context or looking at it from a new angle.

Cynics may say that this re-framing is simply another word for rationalisation. It may be, but so is their cynical view that things are basically negative and that taking a positive outlook should be dismissed as merely a rationalisation. Cynics will interpret even good news in a guarded negative way, as though the whole thing was some kind of plot to draw them into involvement with life, making them vulnerable.

Often this attitude exists because those people want to keep a sense of previous misfortune alive. They want to go on living in the valley of excuses where everyone and everything else has to take the blame. They like to think to themselves, '*I am right to be depressed. I have invested a lot in my experiences. I have earned this depression and I am not going to let some good fortune take it away from me!*'

This mindset is surprisingly widespread in our culture. It is, however, not very effective because, as we have seen, you get more of what you focus on. A negative belief system propagates negative results and creates a vicious circle. Here is where the true value of re-framing can be seen. It breaks into and breaks up the circle.

 A positive belief system puts us in a high State on the Performance Scale. It propagates results which confirm and strengthen our beliefs.

It creates what we can call a **virtuous circle**.

Vicious or Virtuous. Which would you prefer?

THE RULES OF THE GAME

I t is time to set up some of the principles of good design. We already discussed how certain feelings allow us to be at 10, the position on the Performance Scale which we need to reach in order to be truly successful. This State varies from person to person and from situation to situation.

It may be an essential feeling of confidence for one person. It may be a matter of relaxation for another.

It might be both those feelings for the same person at different times.

It might be a combination of the two together. Whatever they may be, we need to know which beliefs will allow us to experience those States.

These beliefs are often called *rules*. We call them that because we all set ourselves criteria which we have to meet before we allow ourselves to have reached the State we want.

We can clarify what we mean by using some practical examples. As was the case of the 'cold calling' lady in the last chapter, what follows is a direct transcript of a conversation between one of the coaches and some of the people in a small group at one of our conferences.

Coach: *We've been talking about success and how, when we're feeling successful, that allows us to be at a 10. What I'm wondering now is, if feeling successful is what allows us to be at a 10, what must happen for us to feel successful. John, what is the answer in your case?*

John: *Well, I suppose I feel successful any time I get recognition for good work and I exceed my monthly sales target.*

Coach: *Thanks, John. How about you, Sue?*

Sue: *Well, I only feel successful when I've had a brilliant day.*

Coach: *And what is a brilliant day for you?*

Sue: *When I've sold to everybody I've seen.*

Coach: *Fine. And finally you over here. It's Frank isn't it?*

Frank: *Yes. I suppose I feel successful when I exceed the expectations of others.*

Coach: *OK. How, for example?*

Frank: *Like finishing a project ahead of time, or maybe producing some original ideas.*

John, Sue and Frank have just told the Coach what their rules are for feeling good. How often did they meet those criteria?

> **Coach:** *OK. John, so how often do you exceed your monthly sales target?*
>
> **John:** *Only about 30% of the time.*
>
> **Coach:** *Does that get you the amount of recognition you want?*
>
> **John:** (laughing slightly) *No, I don't think so.*
>
> **Coach:** *No. And how about you, Sue. How often do you sell to everybody you see?*
>
> **Sue:** *Well, no more than once every two weeks, if that.*
>
> **Coach:** *So how many brilliant days do you have then?*
>
> **Sue:** *Hardly any, I suppose!*

The interesting thing is, there is nothing wrong with the criteria that John and the others are using. Most of us set ourselves similar targets. The difficulty here is that if these are the **only** criteria they use, then they are making it very difficult for themselves to feel successful because they have allowed themselves so few ways to feel good. If that is the case, they may need to re-design their belief systems so that they start working *for* them and not against them.

Coach: *Could we say that the rules you are using are making it very easy to feel failure, and very difficult to feel success, Sue?*

Sue: *Absolutely right. Yes*

Frank: *Yes, I agree too. It can't be denied. I just never looked at it that way before.*

Coach: *Well, since we said that the feeling of success was what put us at a 10, shouldn't we be doing everything we can to make it as easy as possible to feel successful?*

Voice from the Audience: *Hang on a minute!*

Coach: *Sure, no problem. Would you like to make a point?*

Voice: *Well, yes I would. I mean surely all this is*

just a compromise isn't it? A cop out. Isn't it just a lowering of standards? I might as well feel successful just because I get out of bed each morning, mightn't I?

Coach: *Actually I have to say that I think that would be an excellent way to start the day! It's a good question and I can see what you mean. It's true that you could in theory use it to lower your standards. But what we're trying to do here is to use this strategy to enhance performance. The issue is that we have been using rules that make it difficult for us to be successful. And you can only be successful if you feel successful in the first place. If you feel unsuccessful, you become unresourceful and then it's much harder to be successful. See what I mean?*

Voice: (not sounding completed convinced) *I'm not sure.*

Sue: *I think I get it. But then, how would you apply it to my situation here?*

Coach: *Good question! Sounds like an excellent cue for an exercise. We've been through some of your old beliefs. I'd like you to take a few minutes to design yourself some new beliefs that you think might be more helpful to you OK?*

We rejoin the discussion after the exercise has been completed.

Coach: *So, how are we doing here? Frank. Have you designed a new belief, a new rule for yourself?*

Frank: *Yes, I have. I've decided that I will allow myself to feel successful any time I meet my own expectations and have done my best to deliver quality work. Any time I know I'm using my potential, and doing the best with what I know.*

Coach: *Great. How about you, Sue? What new rules have you got to get these brilliant days?*

Sue: *I've decided that it's whenever I'm being of value to my clients, and strengthening my relationship with them. And - oh yes, it wouldn't be too bad to sell to 50% of them as well!* (laughter all round).

Coach: *Excellent. For one thing, that brings a different and better meaning to success, and for another, your new target means that the state you are now allowing yourself to be in is going to get nearer to your old 100% target than when you had to get 100% to feel successful! See what I mean?*

Sue: *I do, yes.*

Coach: (to the Voice) *Is that clearer to you now as well?*

Voice: *I think so. Just run it by me again quickly.*

Coach: *It's just this. When Sue had to get 100% to feel good, she probably got so demoralised by her inability to hit the target that she probably only got say 40%, or less?*

Sue: *Something like.*

Coach: *Whereas now she will move towards her new, more realistic target with the confidence that will actually get her there, and as a result will probably overtake it and score 60%. See what I mean?*

Voice: *Ah, yes! Now I've got it.*

Coach: *That's what allowing yourself to be at a 10 does for your performance!*

That example brings out clearly how well-designed new rules, once reinforced, will allow us to avoid disempowering feelings and access empowering feelings on a daily basis.

So it is up to each of us. To you and to me. Make the commitment to reinforce our new beliefs so that they become part of our sub-conscious selves, like the old beliefs used to be. The difference this time is that now our beliefs will be working *for* us.

OF PAIN AND
PLEASURE

In the last chapter we were concerned with the effects of our ability to change the rules which govern our judgements. There is another parallel area and it is concerned with our pain/pleasure associations which can help to bring about the results we want.

The idea that we can in effect manipulate pain and pleasure once again comes as a surprise to most people. They have always assumed that the two reactions are permanently wired in to our nervous systems. This is not true. As we are beginning to see repeatedly, what has been wired can be re-wired. What has been conditioned can be unconditioned. What has been created can be undone and re-created.

Go back once again to the 'geographically-minded' Salesperson. Although that was only an example, the points arising from it can be applied in any context. However, if you are in Sales and your motivation is the expansion of your client base, but you have a fear of rejection which for you is personal failure, then you have a problem. For you, failure equals pain and your nervous system is trained to avoid pain. You have an internal conflict.

The most skilful strategy is to adjust your pain/pleasure associations. Motivation will not change our association of pain with rejection, but if we stop the automatic association of rejection with failure and instead link it firmly to *feedback*, we can recognise a reason for pleasure. Now things begin to change.

We need to think of rejection as a challenge or a learning experience. Now, as we change what it means to us, we change our belief about it and the pain disappears. Suddenly it becomes much easier to change our habitual behaviour. We get different results and they, in turn, strengthen our new beliefs.

Of course we are not saying that there is no difficulty at all in radically changing ourselves for the better. This is no magic wand. There will always be some element of challenge when we move from our previous traditional comfort zones. So there should be. After all, this book is called 'Breakthrough to Peak Performance' not 'Amble Gently On to Average Performance'! But the heart of the matter is that our challenges are exactly that - challenges, not problems.

There are two sets of questions we must ask ourselves if we are to succeed with the emotional engineering that switches from pain to pleasure.

1. What are the consequences of not taking action? What will it cost me? What is the pain? How does the pain make me feel now?

2. What are the benefits of taking action? What will I gain? What is the pleasure? How does that make me feel now?

Using these powerful questions we can overcome the underlying causes of procrastination and get ourselves to take action. Remember, the willingness to take action distinguishes successful people from the 'also rans'.

Make sure that we have got this clear. The fact is that we will not follow a path to a goal which involves a lot of pain. For example, if my goal is to lose weight, but that will involve exercise which I associate with pain, I may start on the exercise programme but I am unlikely to complete it. I will find excuses for myself. *'It is inconvenient.'* *'I don't have enough time for it.'* I will find myself all too easy to convince!

That is not exactly great design work.

There is no doubt about the power of pain and pleasure as conditioning forces. We need to understand the fact that they control almost all the decisions we make. Generally speaking, we will opt for the choice that will bring pleasure and we will do what we can to avoid pain. What we can do, and what we need to do, is to change what we associate with pain and pleasure.

When we change our ideas and beliefs about what causes pain and what causes pleasure, that will inevitably change our behaviour.

Two examples can illustrate how pain and pleasure are not absolute concepts. One man may love strenuous physical exercise, while another may hate it. The first man enjoys it because he associates it with health, fitness and potential achievement. It gives him pleasure. The other hates it because he associates it with discomfort and inconvenience. It gives him pain. Both men may be experiencing the same physical effects but they have different ideas about what they feel.

Think about a hunger striker who survives a month without food. When we hear the news item about his situation, we think of the pain of starvation, and nobody can doubt that he himself experiences that physical deprivation. However, what sustains him through the ordeal is the belief in the justice of his cause and the attention he is drawing to it. This is his positive view which gives him pleasure which outweighs the pain.

You will often hear people talk of changes they want to make in their lives which somehow they fail to follow through. They feel frustrated and angry with themselves because they cannot get themselves to take the necessary action. They know what they should do and they know why they should do it. Yet they choose not to. Why?

Quite simply they are trying to change their behaviour instead of what *causes* the behaviour. Everyone's life is shaped by what they have *learned* gives them pleasure and what they have *learned* will give them pain. The critical factor in this aspect of our lives is what our past associations would have us believe. The lessons we learn from our past may be different for each of us. There is one lesson which we can all profit from which is to realise the kind of future into which our pain/pleasure conditioned behaviour patterns are leading us.

Charles Dickens' 'A Christmas Carol' provides a perfect parable for Peak Performers.

In the story, the miser Scrooge is taught how to re-wire his pain/pleasure associations in the most dramatic manner by being given a powerful visualisation exercise in which he has to live with his own future. That is of course the direct consequence of his present set of behaviours.

We learned earlier how to pull the future into the present through visualisation so that we can make our desired outcomes reality. Scrooge learned his lesson through a different application of the same exercise. If you are not familiar with the details of the story, get hold of a copy and read it. The impact of the story will make the point very clear. We can all benefit from this lesson at some stage in our lives.

How many schoolchildren avoid doing homework until the last possible moment, thus making a disagreeable job even more unpleasant? How many of us continue to jam rubbish into the swing bin, even though it is so full that the flap does not close and we have to put more effort into pressing it down than it would take to empty it into the big bin at the back door? How many people spend more energy and ingenuity avoiding work than they would use doing it? Do any of these sound familiar?

They are all examples of acting on automatic pilot in the pain/pleasure area. The pain associated with starting the homework, or emptying the bin, or doing the job, has in each case blinded us to the potential pleasure which we would feel once that neccessary task had been completed.

Many automatic reactions control our behaviour. When we are driving and we see a red light we perform a number of behaviours. We slow down. We change gear. We set the hand brake. All without conscious awareness. Our belief that we must slow down and stop - *or experience pain* - triggers these automatic behaviours.

All of these examples are unconscious behaviour patterns provoked by pain/pleasure associations. All of them can be altered by realising the future they will take us into. The ability to envision this future should make us realise that in many cases the avoidance of short term pain guarantees long term pain.

Fortunately what has been learned can be un-learned. We can learn to condition our minds, bodies and emotions to link pain or pleasure to whatever we choose. What is more, by changing what we link pain or pleasure to, we will immediately change our behaviour.

Normally it is not the actual pain or pleasure that drives us. Usually it is the anticipation of pain or pleasure that determines our behaviour. In other words, we are not driven by reality but by our perception of reality.

Perceptions are based on beliefs; beliefs are powered by our internal representational systems and we already know that we can alter those when we choose.

Much productive re-wiring of the pain/pleasure networks can be achieved by running our associations through the 'Scramble' technique which we described on page 89 and 90 in Chapter 8.

Next, in more transcriptions from actual training sessions, are some practical examples which illustrate various points.

Coach: *What do you associate pain with in terms of your working day?*

Mike: *Cold calling*

Andy: *Paper work*

Jenny: *Group presentations*

(Coach writes the answers on a board)

Coach: *OK. And are these things that you really need to do?*

Mike: *Yes.*

Coach: *Right then. What associations do you have to cold calling?*

Mike: *Well, it's tiring. It's unproductive. It can lead to rejection. The company should give me the leads in the first place.*

Coach: *All right. And paper work?*

Andy: *Oh, it's so boring, so tedious, laborious. It seems pointless half of the time. No one ever looks at it.*

Coach: *What about group presentations then?*

Jenny: *Fear of looking stupid in front of clients. Feeling humiliated. Might even lose the client. Risky. It's better one to one.*

Coach: (looking over list) *OK. Well with those associations, it's not surprising that you find it hard to take action. And yet we've all agreed that these are things you have to do, right?*

Mike: *Right.*

Coach: *So what would be the consequences of not taking action - say with regard to cold calling?*

Mike: *Well, there might be no new business. Leads would start to dry up. There would be no expansion.*

Coach: *And paper work?*

Andy: *Well, you'd start to lose track of everything pretty quickly. You'd lose control, become disorganised. There would be no way of checking up on anything, no records. Not very professional, really.*

Coach: *No. And group presentations?*

Jenny: *You might miss major opportunities. Commission. Recognition. Bonuses.*

Coach: *OK - So we've a bit of a challenge here then!*
(general laughter)

Andy: *What's the answer then?*

Coach: *I think there are two things actually. The first is to change the meaning.*

Jenny: *How's that?*

Coach: *Swap the pain/pleasure associations around. Let's go through the list again, but this time make a special effort to give me a positive association for each item. OK? So, once again, cold calling?*

Mike: *Well it's nice to see the appointments getting logged and the diary filling up. You feel you're expanding into the market and seizing opportunity. It's good for the old self-esteem!*

Coach: *Good. And paper work, Andy?*

Andy: *It makes you feel organised and in control. You definitely can plan better, and you feel good when it's done and dusted. I can enjoy doing what I like doing, when I've done what I need to do.*

Coach: *Jenny, what about group presentations?*

Jenny: *Well, you can certainly get a definite buzz out of having an impact on a larger group of people, and influencing higher up the organisation. And there's a sense of accomplishment in meeting a challenge.*

Coach: *All right! So what you can do then is to re-wire the positive associations in place of the negative associations and they become the focus of your attention. And we've been through how to do that - to change the meaning.*

Mike: *Can you really change the meaning just like that? Isn't the meaning just there, regardless of how I may feel about it?*

Coach: *Good question! Let's just try this. Let's say you have just been rejected. What might that mean to you?*
> (indicates each in turn)

Mike: *Well obviously I failed in some way. I blew it!*

Andy: *They don't like me.*

Jenny: *They don't respect me.*

Coach: *Right. Now let's run through it again, only this time give me a positive meaning for the situation, one that might give you the impetus to derive some benefit from the event and take some further action - So - Rejection?*

Mike: *Well, maybe they didn't understand me. I could see it as an opportunity to develop my communication skills.*

Andy: *I could see it as a learning experience. Think about what it tells me about that other person.*

Jenny: *They've rejected the product, not me. It's an opportunity to try out a different approach.*

Coach: *Excellent! So the point is that nothing has any meaning other than the meaning we choose to give to it. So why not choose the meaning which gives us the most benefit, the one most likely to keep us at a 10 and therefore in line for success? As Peak Performers we're interested not just in whether a belief is right or wrong, but whether it limits or empowers us. We can choose.*

Obviously it is not the particular issues that have been covered in these exchanges which are important. The lessons which can be derived from them can be applied to any issue that concerns you. What is important is the principle of re-wiring our associations to pain and pleasure so that they work to our benefit.

Now, just as we did with the Memory Management exercises earlier, it is important that you personalise these ideas for yourself. It is time for an exercise and you need pen and paper.

Exercise 16   Pains in the Neck
First, make a list of all the things you avoid doing, or find difficulty with, but which nonetheless are important for you to do. Be ready to take whatever time you may need to think this through. Be honest with yourself.

Now read the list through and ask yourself about each thing, *'What does this item mean to me? Why do I associate it with pain?'*

Write down the answers beside each item.

Next look at the list again and ask yourself *'What is the positive side to this item? What could or can be good about it?'*

Once again, write down that answer and make the conscious decision to use that positive attitude and its associated 'pleasure' every time the situation comes up in the future.

Incidentally, this new viewpoint and re-framing may show you an instant solution to some long-running difficulty. If that happens, **act at once**. Strike while the iron is hot. The pleasure you will get from crossing it off from your list will prove the validity of what we have been saying.

We talked earlier about your position as a car driver. We can take that metaphor further by suggesting that your belief is your car and it will only run if it is supported by its wheels. For any belief, the wheels are the references which it has to reality. Both good and bad beliefs rely on these references.

Try another quick exercise.

Exercise 17   Unbelievable

Choose from among the disempowering beliefs of your own which you must have identified as you read what we have been saying. Write down a list of the references which support that belief.

Take a good long look at those references. It is quite likely that most of them are historical, coming from away back in your past when you were ready to accept other people's directions.

Some of them may have been collected from people that you well know to be biased. Some may have been based on early self-doubts which you have now grown out of. The more you examine them and test their reliability, the more likely those wheels are to fall off the vehicle and the disempowering belief itself will begin to collapse.

Exercise 18   Now Hear This!

Now set out to build the new belief which will replace the old one and which will work for you. It must be empowering in the same area as the one which you are discarding. Make another list. This time make the list of all the reasons why the new belief should be true. Go through that new list and dig into it to produce more evidence to support the new belief.

Remember 'Modelling'? Think about people you respect or admire who already demonstrate this new belief. Find out their references and make sure that you build them into your own new structure.

When you have done all that, take a step back for a moment and have a look at this new you and how this new belief really suits you. Before you know it, you may find someone else using you as a model for themselves. When that happens, remember to be as generous as you expected your models to be to you.

JUST IMAGINE

The power of belief is really the power of our imagination.

Last year we met a very nervous presenter at a convention. He could hardly hold onto his notes because his hands were shaking so badly. It was obvious that his anxiety was directly linked to a belief that he was going to fail.

We asked him why he felt so nervous and it turned out that he was already imagining his failure quite vividly. He could hear his boss criticising him. He could see the audience looking bored. He could feel their attention wandering. What we had to do was to ask him to imagine things differently.

We told him to imagine how it would feel if everything went right and to talk positively to himself about succeeding. He knew how much work he had done on his presentation. We told him to imagine his boss congratulating him. And to get him off to a good start, we told him that when he heard the other speakers at the Convention being applauded, he should imagine that applause was for him.

It worked. It was bound to, once he put his imagination to positive use.

!

The point is, if you remember, that as far as your brain and nervous system are concerned **there is no difference between a real or a vividly imagined event**. That is why advertisements are so powerful. They use highly sensual materials - both sounds and pictures - to create sensations of pleasure which you link to the product. They create the belief that you will benefit from it. Marketing professionals would not be spending tens of thousands or even many millions of pounds on advertising if it did not work.

Of course advertisements work because they put incredibly powerful 'movies' in your mind. Those are effective because that is just the way your mind works.

Once again, think about any strongly held belief of your own. You will discover, as in the last chapter, that it has powerful emotional links to your memory and your imagination. Those links were probably forged long ago and very often by someone with the best intentions, like the mother who told her daughter not to talk to strangers. Most of us do not consciously choose our beliefs whether they are strong, positive and empowering or negative and limiting.

This is why it is so important to learn how to select our own beliefs and to choose those empowering ones.

For instance, when you see an attractive person who smiles at you, how do you react? Do you ask yourself '*Is that a welcoming smile?*', or do you ask yourself if they are going to laugh in your face? It is easy to see which belief is the better one to choose! Yet our old beliefs may have created habits which continually prevent us from seizing opportunities.

We need a strategy that will help us to stay focused and create a level of certainty and expectation which will keep us going, even when we do not have the experiences or the references to support us. We can learn to use the visualisation techniques which are often part of an athlete's training plans.

A classic example is that of Roger Bannister who used his imagination to create the belief and the certainty in his nervous system that it was possible to break the 'four-minute mile' barrier. There were no references to suggest that it could be done. But he achieved it by seeing it happen in fine detail over and over again in his imagination.

Perhaps the most fascinating fact is that, once Bannister had broken the four-minute barrier, everyone's reference points were changed. Other athletes began to do the same thing, until nowadays it has become an almost commonplace standard.

There is an important lesson for us in that fact. These athletes were not suddenly endowed with new physical abilities, but with a new *attitude*. They had the latent potential all the time. Once they seriously believed that they could run the four-minute mile, they could. Henry Ford put the whole thing very succinctly when he said:

'Whether you think you can or whether you think you can't, you're probably righ!.'

All these athletes began saying that they *could*. They visualised the achievement. Athletes often use this visualisation technique in their preparation. They will replay what they have actually done and then deliberately alter their internal film show, improving it where they can. They think about what happened, they change the visualisation. The technique is not complex but the benefits can be enormous.

Equally, past experience, left to itself, tends to result in more of the same. Habits repeat themselves. Revisualising a previous bad experience leads us to expect the same thing to happen again and expectation tends to be fulfilled. You get more of what you focus on. A negative belief repeated over and over builds up its own momentum until it becomes unstoppable and unquestionable.

But that is only because we do not question it!

We should learn from the athletes that things can be put into reverse, and that self-nourishing positive beliefs can grow just as effectively as negative ones. The athletes look at the old performance in their minds and change it. They operate on it by using their imagination and bring the new improved version into the present.

Transforming the past through the present is another incredibly powerful revolutionary idea. Realise that the point of power is always *in the present - now*. Far too many people allow themselves to assume that they are helpless victims of the past. We know that we can liberate ourselves from the past by changing our beliefs. Perhaps the most liberating realisation is that you *can* choose to change in this way; you can transform the past and you have the resources you need to do these things already *within yourself*.

It really is easy. What you have to realise is that you have been doing it all your life, without being aware that you can take control. Now that you know you can take control, do it consciously. Picture your goals and make them compelling. Live out your imagination because that is where your potential is to be found.

When you change your beliefs about what is possible you will actually change what is possible and you will transform your results.

We are discussing specific techniques for **Belief** management. They are parallel to the techniques of **State** management, which we looked at earlier. It is important to realise that the same patterns are at work.

For example, we have been talking about refusing to be controlled by limited and limiting mental filmshows based on early conditioning. These movies are based on beliefs which are also conditioned and which have been edited and re-edited over the years. Beliefs can act as filters either to include or screen out evidence. If we are filtering out evidence to the contrary, we can feel absolutely certain about anything at all.

Exercise 19   Effervescence!

Consider the following sentence:

> *'Peak Performance is the result of laser-like focus, adopting the fizzy of certainty and operating from maps that guide us toward the achievement of our desired outcomes.'*

Now answer this question. How many times does the letter 'F' appear in that sentence?

However many you think there are, just go back and check. Unless you are one of a very small minority, your answer will be different the second time. That may not seem important, but actually it is - very. Have a read through this genuine conversation recorded at one of our training sessions.

Coach: *Well, that's what's written on the card. Some of you must be surprised to discover that you all had the same card.*

Tony: *Yes, that's right, how can we have? We've all got different answers!*

Coach: *Frank, is your card exactly the same as John's?*

Frank: *Well, yes. I didn't think it could be, but yes, it's the same words.*

Coach: *But John's got seven 'F's' and you've only got three.*

Frank: *I know.*

Coach: *So he's got to be wrong, hasn't he?*

Frank: *He must be wrong, yes.*

Coach: *Are you absolutely certain that there are only three 'F's' on the card?*

Frank: *Yes I am. There can't be more than three. I went through the card quite a few times.*

Coach: *So, you are so certain that you'd be willing to bet some money on it?* (Tongue-in-cheek)

Frank: *Sure.*

Coach: *All right. What sort of money? A tenner?*

Frank: *Oh yes. Make it £50.*

Coach: *£50! And John, you say you've got seven 'F's' on your card. Are you certain about that?*

John: *Yes, I am.*

Coach: *And it's the same card as Frank's?*

John: *Apparently.*

Coach: *So will you match Frank's bet then?*

John: *I will. Yes!*

As you read that, with whom were you identifying? Frank or John? Or maybe you think they were both wrong! Whatever your answer to that, your sense of certainty would be the same and just as strong as their's. Actually, it was John who was right and we were able to prove it to Frank before he got as far as taking out his wallet.

The interesting point is that, in general terms, neither Frank nor John was more intelligent or more observant than the other. But Frank was filtering some of the letters out of his perception. This was largely because the letter 'F' in words like 'of' does not sound like an 'F'. It sounds like a 'V', and that was the way Frank was representing it to himself. Once he did that, his perception was blocked and he was convinced of the correctness of the limiting belief that there were only three 'F's' in the sentence.

We asked John how he found all seven straight away, and he said:

> '*Well at first I managed to tell myself to question everything right from the beginning. That helped me to find four 'F's'. Then I got stuck for a while until I suddenly hit on the idea of holding the card upside down. Suddenly I could see all the 'F's' quite clearly.*'

 What is the crucial difference between Frank and John? The answer is that **John is more flexible - a crucial Peak Performance skill**. By the way, John's idea of holding the card upside down was surely a stroke of genius. Our **con**ceptions govern our **per**ceptions and when John turned his card upside down, he momentarily put his conditioned conceptual mind on hold.

Deprived of conditioned knowledge the mind was able to see clearly what was really the case. Once he had stopped seeing what he believed, John was able to believe what he actually saw. 'Already knowing' can be a great hindrance to learning.

Betty Edwards is the author of 'Drawing on the Right Side of the Brain' - possibly the most influential book on the skill of drawing ever published. She hit on the same strategy. When she saw that some of her students were copying drawings by old masters, she did not stop them. She did not discourage the practice, but she did require the students to turn the reproductions they were trying to copy upside down, before going to work.

The result was massively improved copies, and for the same reason that John was more accurate than Frank. Freed from what the students thought they *already knew* beforehand about the shapes, they were more free to *see* the shapes in front of them.

All this goes to show that we tend to see the world as *we* are, not as *it* is. It is true that you cannot go through life turning the world upside down or standing on your head every few minutes.

However, you can achieve much the same effect through flexibility and through developing an awareness of our tendency to filter the evidence to fit in with our established outlook.

> Two people, one a young mother and the other a driving instructor are standing beside each other waiting to cross the road. They both witness an accident in which a small child is hit by a car. They both see the event from exactly the same position.
>
> Afterwards, one of them remembered almost every detail about the child, its sex, age, hair colour and clothing, and very little else. The other recalled the child as a blur, but remembered almost every detail about the car - its make, colour, registration number and so on.

There are no prizes for guessing which witness was which. They both filtered out things outside their usual area of focus.

In another situation, assume you work with a colleague called Mike. You regard him as a nice person and you like him a lot. One day Mike arrives at work, but when you ask him how things are going, he frowns and tells you to get lost. What is your reaction? You probably think he must be having a bad day. You probably even feel sympathetic.

Now, instead, suppose Mike is someone you do not like. Suppose you think he is very unpleasant and hard to get on with. One day when you arrive for work, *this* Mike asks *you* how things are going. What is your reaction? You probably suspect him of being up to something. You may even tell him to get lost!

In both cases, it is the same sort of thing. You filter the significance of Mike's behaviour to fit in with what you already believe about him. Try re-reading the examples and assume that the 'you' in the story are two different people but Mike is the same person in both stories. Something similar will happen. People filter evidence according to established beliefs. In advanced stages this produces prejudice or bigotry.

The man from Decca who rejected the Beatles was operating from a belief that there was no future for groups with a line-up of three guitars and drums. Because of his belief, he was able to filter out whatever his senses and awareness might have been telling him about the outstanding originality of the band.

Frogs eat flies. Put a frog in a jar full of dead flies and what have you got? A very happy frog, presumably! Actually you will soon have a dead frog! Frogs are conditioned to go into action on the perception of movement. Dead flies do not move, so the frog starves.

Take other examples, in reverse.

An inventor was woken up in the night because one of the mattress springs had come loose and was digging into his side. This is something an average insomniac would try to filter out of awareness, if at all possible. Not so with our inventor. He thought about the shape of the spring and as a result invented the new flexible egg-cup based on the shape. You may have seen one. They became a viable commercial product.

The man who invented the revolving bullet chamber for the six-gun got the idea from watching the great paddle wheels on the Mississippi steam-boats. He just transposed the idea into another domain. He had a flexibility that did not filter out creative ideas.

Exercise 20   Drive Me Dotty

You may be familiar with the exercise with the nine dots.

•   •   •

•   •   •

•   •   •

The challenge is to link all the dots together using only four straight lines and without lifting your pen or pencil from the paper. If you are not familiar with the puzzle have a go at it. It would be wise to try it on a separate piece of paper.

Our answer and the conclusions we draw from it can be found in the Appendix at the back of the book.

The solution is not the really important thing. What is important is the fact that when we let go of the original fixed belief - 'It can't be done!' - then all kinds of things become possible. We have worked with groups of twenty or thirty people on the nine dot challenge. Over the thirty minutes we allow for it, it has often taken as much as twenty-five minutes for someone to come up with the answer.

Interestingly enough, once that has happened, other possible solutions are often proposed in the remaining five minutes. To let you off the hook about what other solutions might be, they include making the dots bigger so that in effect you can cheat a bit!

Anthropologist and biologist Lyall Watson, in his book 'Lifetide', tells a remarkable story about a tribe of monkeys living on an island near Japan. A new food, freshly dug sweet potatoes, was introduced to the group, placed on the sandy beach near where they lived. The monkeys' usual food required no preparation and to begin with they were reluctant to eat the potatoes which were covered in earth and sand. However one monkey overcame the difficulty by washing the potatoes in a nearby river. She taught others what to do. This was highly advanced 'monkey business', more complex than their other conscious behaviours.

The truly remarkable thing was what happened next. After about a hundred monkeys had learned the technique and the new behaviour, other monkeys who had no contact with the first tribe at all, even living on another island, began to do the same thing.

Lyall Watson's discovery came to be known as the 100th monkey syndrome. It is completely outside known laws of cause and effect. But it did happen. Various thinkers have been trying to account for this sort of phenomenon for decades. Jung even invented the name 'synchronicity' to describe these sequences of events which seem meaningfully connected, but in such a way that we cannot explain in terms of usual laws.

Think back to the behaviour of the Peak Performer in the five steps of the **DANCE** model. 1. Have a **D**esired outcome. 2. Take **A**ction. 3. **N**otice the results. 4. **C**hange. 5. Model **E**xcellence.

The 100th monkey, who was obviously a Peak Performer, followed this model.

We know that successful people are those who can get themselves to take Action, the second step. But the step which calls for true resourcefulness is the fourth, Change. How do we stay positive and make the necessary changes if the results are discouraging, confusing or threatening? To start with, we need to work at staying at a 10. There is one thing more than anything else which allows us to stay there. It is belief.

Constantly arriving change can look hazardous and threatening. It certainly is unpredictable. Many of us find that it makes us feel insecure.

Peak Performers do not see things like that. Where others see threats, they see opportunities. They understand that the element of serendipity in life is what makes it creative, challenging and fun. They do not allow fixed beliefs to block their awareness. They do not allow insecurity to take over their lives, because they know that reality does not always arrive in neatly wrapped packages.

Peak Performers allow themselves to be in harmony with reality, however it develops. They become linked to an increasingly creative and rewarding chain of development. Some call it luck. Some call it synchronicity. Peak Performers have been known to call it unconscious competence.

When we are organising training sessions on 'The Power of Belief' we involve people in a physical metaphor to take them beyond current limiting beliefs. We coach people to break through a piece of wooden board with the palm of their hand!

The interesting thing is that at the start of the day most people believe that they cannot do it. They are sure they are not strong enough or they suspect it involves some secret technique. Strength is not the issue, and although it is true that technique counts for something, the real point is that the people concerned break through the board when they give themselves the mental permission to do so.

What was at issue was self belief, and the central element in the technique is the visualisation exercise in which each of the people is encouraged to 'see' the hand passing through and beyond the board.

They allow themselves to get into a good State. They give the board a meaning. They associate pleasure with the successful outcome of breaking it. They visualise themselves as having broken through. Suddenly, they adopt a psychological certainty. It becomes possible.It is a great metaphor.

 You transcend limiting beliefs by seeing past them. Remember the goal is not an end in itself, it is a target to facilitate the unfolding of our potential. The journey is what really counts.

As far as breaking through the board is concerned, the important thing is breaking through the hesitation or doubt you may feel. Breaking through fear, or procrastination or whatever is holding you up, is all that successful people do.

They get themselves to take action where others do not. They may not always get the results they originally expected, but they see every result as a learning opportunity and are ready to take whatever new action their belief in their goal will require.

Peak Performers have flexibility in their belief systems. They do not rule things out as impossible because they have not been done before. They are willing to redesign and reframe themselves. They are the people who break through boards, or break the four-minute mile.

Each of them will have an individual 'barrier' which their belief will empower them to overcome.

As they unfold their potential they become an inspiration to the 100th monkey that lurks within all of us!

BREAKTHROUGH
TO
PEAK PERFORMANCE

Part Four

RAPPORT

WORDS, WORDS, WORDS

In the first three parts of this book we have been dealing with what we call the inner game. We were concentrating on learning how you can improve your own performance. We looked at State, Belief, Imagination, Focus and Physiology all with a view to helping you know how you could take control and change many things which for years you had believed to be set in stone.

You were learning how to communicate with yourself in the most effective way. It is essential that you do begin with yourself. It is part of the inside-out approach. If you want to change the world, even if it is only your own world, you have to start by changing you. Once you have made that commitment to yourself, you are ready to move on. You will find that as you learn to communicate effectively with yourself, you will automatically begin to communicate more effectively with other people.

Although this improvement will begin to develop almost automatically, there are some fascinating new skills to acquire which will help. Once you have made the commitment to it, communication with yourself is relatively straightforward. After all, we have immediate access to our own thoughts, feelings and experiences. However, when it comes to contact and communication with other people, we can only achieve that by reaching their thoughts, feelings and experiences. It is of course a two-way process involving language, behaviour and physiology.

Language and behaviour are the communication systems we use to convey our thoughts and feelings to each other. So our access to each other's inner worlds has to be in some ways an indirect affair. Everything depends on our ability to interpret the signals we are receiving and the other person's ability to interpret those we are sending out. The most powerful of all achievements are those we achieve together.

Working together can be a complicated process. To begin with, not everybody shares the same ideas about the meanings of words. Far from it! The variance is far greater than most of us realise. People who take part in our training sessions are often amazed by the variations given to the implications of everyday words.

Exercise 21   Don't Spare Your Blushes

Before you read on, take a piece of paper and write down ten words which you personally associate with the word 'sex'. Write what you like. You do not have to show it to anyone else!

N.B. If this little exercise is to have any meaning in your understanding of this part of the book it is important that you carry it out now, before you read the next few paragraphs.

When we run our training sessions, we divide the participants into groups, usually of five people, and ask them, individually, to write down a list of ten words which they associate with a given word. We often use the words 'sex' or 'learning'. What follows is a transcript of a typical example.

Coach: *Right, OK, everyone finished? Let's see now, we've got three groups of five people here, so that's five times ten words, that's fifty. So each group will have produced fifty words. All in relation to the key word 'sex'! So this should be interesting! Let's see what you've got in common then. Fred, you've collected and checked everyone's words from your group. What are your findings?*

Fred: *Unbelievable! I wouldn't have believed it anyway. We had not one single word in common!*

Coach: *How many other of you groups had the same result? All of you! Seems a bit unlikely doesn't it? Let's have some examples. Alison, would you mind sharing your words with everyone else?*

Alison: *I've written 'feminism, danger, beauty, love, hate, relationship, flirtation, forbidden, smile and babies!'*

Coach: *OK, Alison, thanks for sharing that. And how about you, Fred?*

Fred: *Er, well, rather different! I've got 'Enjoyment, affairs, secrecy, sensual, sucking* (laughter from audience), *breasts, legs, bums* (more laughter) *power and embrace'. Yes, well obviously my mind works a little differently from Alison's!*

Coach: *Just ever so slightly! Yes!*

Frank: *Well I hope so anyway.*

Coach: *Absolutely. That's what this exercise is designed to show. Twenty different words. For something I know you all think about most of the time! And you said the other thirty were all different as well!*

The second group's lists were just as varied. With the three groups producing one hundred and fifty words altogether, one or two words were similar from one group to another. However, as we usually find, it is very unusual for any group to have more than a couple of words in common. Perhaps that is not surprising. It reflects something that happens all the time.

Incidentally, before we move on, how did your own list compare with the two in the transcript? You can try the experiment with a group of friends or colleagues and check the results.

Another illustration arises in what happened with an English secretary who was working for a Canadian boss. He could not understand why she always appeared to be rather downcast.

Eventually he asked her about it. He was astonished when she said that he depressed her by always asking what was wrong. He could not remember ever asking that.

It turned out that he always greeted her with the words *'Hi! What's up?'* Remember, he was a Canadian. Where he came from, the expression *'What's up?'* meant *'What's going on?'* or *'What's happening?'* On the other hand, the English girl always thought of the question *'What's up?'* as asking *'What's the matter?'* or *'What's wrong?'* Not surprisingly, she was depressed by the constant repetition. The discussion between them soon solved the problem.

Obviously the gap between **Us** and **Them** is a good example of the tricky territory which exists between our first and second creations!

Dealing with **Us** is one thing. Dealing with **Them** seems to offer a much more awesome challenge. This is especially true because even our main communication system - language - requires such skilful handling. We will be showing you how to handle it with great skill in due course.

First we should point out that the gap between communicating with ourselves - sometimes referred to as **intra**-personal - and communicating with others - which we call **inter**-personal - is not exactly the Grand Canyon! It is actually quite easy to build bridges between these two worlds. We would be living in a truly bizarre world if it were not.

Both worlds operate in terms of representational systems. Language itself is one. We have already worked on how to manage some of the systems.

Indeed, some of the techniques we have already examined can be used with any necessary modifications to build two-way bridges between ourselves and other people.

It might help if we distinguished between the intra-personal world and the inter-personal world by thinking of the first in terms of the metaphor which we have already set up. We can call it a 'mental movie'. Now we can think of the second in terms of 'theatre'. This is because we are dealing with the dramatic space which we share with other people on the stage of the world which contains us all.

Walt Disney was a master at working at the interface between these two worlds. It is interesting to notice how so many of the Peak Performers from the past whom we refer to had such an intuitive grasp of many of the instruments in the 'orchestra' which we are building up.

Think about what Walt Disney actually did when he made his early films. Not only were they almost outrageously original - for example, they included the first full-length animations ever made. They were highly personal. They were the products of an extravagant visionary and they were all developed from within the depths of one man's intra-personal system.

That in itself is perhaps not all that unusual. Most artists are like that. However most artists do not go on with total confidence to project their vision at the public as viable commercial propositions, risking millions of dollars in the ventures.

What made Walt Disney so sure that his work would be so well received?

The answer is that Disney had a strategy. It was a brilliant strategy of course. But it was simple. We can all use it for our own purposes. Disney represented the inter-personal world to himself in terms of his own intra-personal system.

It worked like this. He viewed the project such as the idea for the new movie from three different positions and in terms of those three different attitudes.

First of all Disney would run the whole movie through his mind as the **Artist**. At this stage, he would not compromise. Like any poet or painter in an ivory tower, he dreamed the dream exactly as he, and only he, wanted to dream it. He made the world over in the image of his own desire.

Next he would, as it were, step aside from the dream and he would look at it and study it from the point of view of the **Realist**. Now he was asking himself what it was going to take to make the dream happen. Notice the question. It was not could this dream be made to happen - not even from the Realist's point of view - but how could it be made to happen!

From this position, Uncle Walt was anything but an idealistic dreamer. He was the hard-bitten pragmatist, balancing budgets and building teams of hands-on craftsmen who would bring the vision into reality.

Finally came the master-stroke as Disney moved into yet another and a third position, that of the **Critic**.

From this point of view he would run the film through his mind yet again, as though it were the finished production, and he was a hostile reviewer on opening night. He would look for weaknesses in his own representation.

If he saw any deadwood in it, out it would go, no matter what the level of his own personal attachment to it. At this stage he was prepared to be quite ruthless and it was the secret of his success. It explains his popularity and his confidence. He had the precious gift of being able to see himself and his ideas as others would see them and he was prepared to deal honestly with what he saw. This was the fundamental basis of his ability to communicate.

We recommend this three-step process in the art of building the rainbow bridges between ourselves and other people.

Artist, Realist and Critic.

Cover the ground from these three points of view and you have a recipe for success which is about as failsafe as you can get. If you think about it, you will realise that the first position is taken from the point of view of what we called **Leadership** in Chapter 3 while the other two positions deal with the **Management** view.

Exercise 22   Dare to be a Disney!

Take any project which you have in mind. It does not have to be anything as ambitious as making a feature film! It could just as easily be the planning of a family holiday or a suggestion you want to make in a meeting in the workplace. Run it through this three-step process. Disney himself used the same technique in other contexts. In his own meetings he would notice which of the three positions was most lacking in the views being expressed by the other people present. Then he himself would immediately make up the deficiency by taking up that position and applying it to the project.

When Disney created his movies for the first time in his mind from the Artist's position, he took things a step further.

He looked at the film from the viewpoint of each of the characters which he was creating in turn. What is more, he then instructed his animators to draw each character from the feeling which he had derived from that viewpoint.

Imagine how much more impact **you** are going to have in what we have called the theatre of the world if you run through any future scenario including yourself, from the point of view of the other people who are going to be involved.

See yourself as you are going to be seen!

If it turns out that you have imagined it all wrong, what have you got? - Exactly! - You will have fantastic feedback for yourself. You will have a brilliant learning opportunity.

Now reflect on what you have learned. Remember the DANCE of Life. Dance your new situation like Walt Disney did. You will have taken a giant step on the road to becoming a great communicator.

Walt Disney succeeded in getting people to buy into his vision of Snow White. Taking on "The Terminator' might be another matter! However, the greater the challenge, the greater the opportunity.

Arnold Schwarznegger's 'Terminator' character is a great personification of all the things we fear about other people - their possible hostility, their unpredictability, the problems we have with negotiating or communicating with them.

Exercise 23   Wrestling with Arnie

On our training course, we sometimes play a game with the participants which is in fact an exercise with a serious purpose. Try it for yourself. Once again you will need pencil and paper.

First of all choose someone with whom you would like to have a better relationship. This needs to be someone who really causes you problems. This is your 'Arnie'.

Now holding this book and your paper and pencil in your hand, position yourself in what we call your first position. Visualise the Arnie you have chosen. How do you feel when you have to go and negotiate with that person? Make a list of the various feelings that come to mind when you think about your Arnie. To help you, it might contain words like 'frustrated', 'fearful' or 'resentful'. You know your own feelings.

When you have done that move to position two. It helps if you actually physically move, sometimes even to the extent of going into another room. In this new space step into Arnie's shoes. Use your imagination and ask yourself how he or she feels about meeting you! Make another list of those ideas. You may be surprised at how similar they are. Perhaps your Arnie is looking at an Arnie too!

Finally, move to a third position and become a consultant you have paid to come and help sort out the situation. The consultant puts two questions:

   1. What is happening here?
   (a) Is there no trust?
   (b) Is there no listening?
   (c) Are there lots of presumptions?

2. What can you do to improve matters?

If you get stuck on that one, the consultant will push you by asking you a question you have heard before, earlier in this book.

*'All right, if you don't know the answer, ask yourself what you might come up with if you **did** know the answer?'* - and do not let yourself run away from **that** challenge. You will realise how useful this question is when someone is avoiding an issue.

When you have completed the exercise, you may be surprised that you have learnt how to change your image of Arnie. You realise that Arnie can be your greatest teacher.

What do Arnies teach us that no-one else does? They reveal in no uncertain fashion just how well or how badly we are performing as a communicator.

After an encounter with Arnie, we know just how much or how little emotional mastery we have over ourselves. We begin to be able to recognise our fear, our anger, our impatience and all those other things which get in the way and make our Arnie into an Arnie in the first place. Arnie is the best feedback system any of us can get.

Looking back for a moment, the story of the Canadian boss and his secretary is a classic example of different words meaning different things to different people. But words are a remarkably small part of the communication process. Research indicates that the sound or tone of the voice has more to do with the process than the words themselves. Psychological research suggests that the words account for as little as 7% of what we communicate, whereas the tone carries as much as 38% of the meaning.

When your mother called your name, you could usually tell if she was worried about you, or wondered where you were, or had good news or if you definitely were getting no sweets that day!

That thought will begin to explain the point we are making. What follows is a simple but clear indication of how emphasis can change the meaning of an apparently simple sentence.

Consider these words. *'I never said that he stole the money.'*

Now read that sentence again, in each case putting a heavy stress on the word in italics and see what happens to the meaning:

1. *I* never said that he stole the money.
   (The implication is clear. Someone else said it.)

2. I *never* said that he stole the money.
   (Again it is quite clear. The speaker is denying an responsibility for the accusation.)

3. I never *said* that he stole the money.
   (The speaker suggests that the implication was made some other way.)

4. I never said that *he* stole the money.
   (Presumably somebody else must have.)

5. I never said that he *stole* the money.
   (Perhaps he just borrowed it and intended to put it back.)

6. I never said that he stole the *money*.
   (Perhaps not, but he may have taken something else that is missing!)

It is interesting how a change of stress can give a simple eight word sentence six quite different meanings **which no-one will fail to understand.**

You may have wondered what happened to the missing 55% of our communication. You will quite probably be surprised to learn that it goes to our physiology!

Our gestures, our facial expressions, our posture all combine to command the lion's share. To accept these figures you must remember that when we talk about what is communicated, we are talking about what is **received**. It is vital that the point is understood. If it is not, then this book is failing to communicate to you, the reader!

It is no good just delivering words if you are not being understood. It is pointless and it can be destructive, like a man shouting at a dog. You can say whatever you like to your dog, but, when you shout your message at it, all it will hear is **shouting,** because the tone of your voice carries a stronger message than any words.

Elements of Verbal Communication

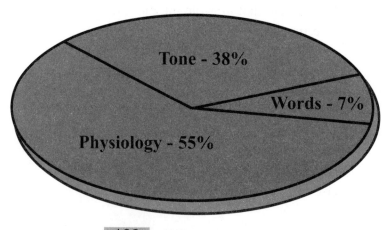

Tone - 38%

Words - 7%

Physiology - 55%

The same principle applies to a teacher and a pupil, or a boss and an employee, or any two people trying to communicate. Unless you need the volume to carry a great distance, shouting indicates a loss of control, and that is the message which gets through to the person at the receiving end. That is what they will remember.

Probably the most familiar example is the archetypal Englishman abroad.

> He stops at a petrol station, say in Spain, and after filling the tank, he asks for directions. Of course he speaks in English. The Spanish pump attendant's reply is a shrug of the shoulders, and speaking no English, he spreads his hands and say '*Que*?' The Englishman's response is to repeat the question twice as loudly but with no greater success! Eventually he drives off obviously thinking 'bloody stupid Spaniards', while the Spaniard stands there with a look which clearly states his sentiments 'aggressive lunatic Englishman!'

That is not just a caricature. We saw exactly that scenario played out only last year when we were in Spain ourselves.

That picture is an exaggerated example of what can happen all too often when people try to communicate a message without realising that things can go wrong, because we are unconscious of the way we communicate. Tone and body language are often unconsciously added to the verbal message. Once we are aware of their importance, we can take more control of how we use them. It is effort well spent if we concentrate on managing the communication process.

In Part 4, we are concerned with **Rapport**. That may not be a word that we use too often in ordinary conversation, but it is an extremely valuable social skill which most successful people have mastered. They realise that working well with others produces the best results because it empowers both us and them.

The foundation stone for everything which rapport makes possible is *trust*.

We regularly ask people what they believe to be the principal benefits that arise from rapport. Their replies make interesting reading and include many positive ideas such as mutual co-operation, quicker achievement of goals, better understanding, social enjoyment and so on. However, time after time it is that word *trust* which comes to the top of the list.

In communication, trust is the difference that makes the difference. Where trust goes up, barriers come down and all kinds of things become possible.

Some managers find it impossible to delegate and spend much of their time dictating solutions to their employees. They then attract other people's problems and get the blame arising from them. In the same way they try to pass on the blame when their own situations go wrong. They are in a lose/lose situation arising from lack of trust. They live in a culture of blame and of buck-passing. Their 'communication' boils down to '*Listen to me!*' They fail to realise that their lack of trust creates a reciprocal resentment.

Employees in these situations quickly lose any sense of loyalty or belonging. Their thinking runs along lines beginning '*If he doesn't trust me, why should I bother?*'

Trust needs to be a two-way street. While the manager must learn to delegate and trust the person involved, that same person needs to respect and trust the manager when a decision has to be taken at that level.

In a trusting environment, where rapport has been established, other people's decisions very seldom come as a shattering surprise.

When you have mastered your motivation and mastered the powers of belief, you start to trust yourself. That level of self-confidence is necessary before you can begin to trust others. When we reach that stage, we will find ourselves surrounded by independent but co-operative people who set their own goals to everyone's mutual benefit. This is rapport at full throttle! High achievers are self-led.

Managers have to be like that before they can create teams like that. They have to start by talking less and listening more. They have to pay more attention to the needs of others.

Managers need to learn to listen.

Parents have to become like that before they can expect children to be like that. They have to broadcast less and pay more attention to the needs of others.

Parents need to learn to listen.

Sales people have to be like that if they want to sell effectively. They have to broadcast less and pay more attention to the needs of others.

Sales people need to learn to listen.

People in any relationship, and that surely includes everybody everywhere, need to be like that if they want to be successful - which means that the relationship itself is successful. Everyone needs to talk less and to broadcast less and to pay more attention to the needs of others.

Everyone needs to learn to listen!

You will gather that this is quite important! Being like that is a matter of rapport. Therefore the next thing we ask is **how** do we develop this skill of rapport. This is the skill which makes great coaches, great managers, great entertainers, great sales people, great parents, great lovers - the list is endless.

So how is it done? After all, it is easy to have rapport with people like us. We tend to like people who are like ourselves. But how do we establish rapport with people who have different values, different skills, different interests, different education, different nationality or different beliefs? Remember we cannot always choose the people we work with.

TECHNIQUE -

VARIATIONS ON A

THEME

Most of our actions are automatic and unconscious, but we have seen and understood that by becoming conscious of them we can effect positive and beneficial change. This is particularly true when we are dealing with our interactions with other people. Most of our goals involve other people, therefore anything we can do to improve relationships can only be beneficial. Behaving skilfully in our relationships is the science of '**Rapport**'.

Once we become aware of the driving forces behind our own behaviour, we gain the power to take control. In the same way when we become aware of what drives other people, we can help **them** take control. We can then move on to destinations we both want to reach. Most particularly we can move on to goals and destinations we can only reach together.

Rapport is a two-way effect. We help ourselves by using the resources we find in others, while at the same time making sure that what we do is for their benefit as well. Peak Performers are only interested in 'win/win' relationships and outcomes.

Earlier on, we concentrated on improving **ourselves**, by learning to take control. Now as we move to consider rapport, we are firmly in terrain which involves others.

We are moving from the inner game to the outer game where we need to master communication through understanding and controlling our shared external systems. This involves '**Pacing**' which deals with understanding and '**Leading**' which concerns control. We will examine both these technical concepts later.

The essential principle remains the same. We began the inner game by learning to take responsibility for ourselves. We begin the outer game by taking responsibility in our relationships.

Within ourselves we discovered the crucial value of flexibility. It is surely not surprising that it is an even more valuable asset when we are dealing with others.

Flexibility can be called '**The Law of Requisite Variety**'. It is absolutely essential, because we can never guarantee how other people may behave, and we must be ready to adjust our response to any situation. Whoever has the most flexibility or the widest range of responses will remain in control of the system or the relationship.

Think of it this way. If you have a client who has **fifteen** ways of resisting or blocking his awareness of your brilliant new idea but you have the flexibility to generate **sixteen** ways of creating new awareness, you stand the better chance of deciding the outcome of your negotiations. If you can make just one more move than the other person, then you have the requisite variety for the relationship.

The skill is increasingly to expand your range and there are means to that end.

> ☆ **Become aware.**
> ☆ **Take responsibility.**
> ☆ **Be flexible.**

If you use your skills at rapport for exploitation, your gains will only be short term, and those who see what you are up to will have no hesitation in using the same techniques on you! As you sow, so shall you reap. The path of Peak Performance constantly reinforces our sense of such basic moral laws, which govern all our actions in this world.

When people meet resistance from each other, the standard response is usually just to push harder against each other. The result is conflict and the outcome is win/lose at best or more often lose/lose. It is an inelegant strategy. We might take the oriental art of Ju-Jitsu, or Aikido, as a more skilful model. Here the opponent's strength is used to bring about an overcoming of his resistance or aggression.

There is a parallel in the way in which a Peak Performer will use the skill of rapport. Rather than bludgeoning the other person in a doomed attempt to **make** them see our point of view, we use their energy to achieve positive change. We work **with** their energy, not against it. We first of all make a change in **ourselves**, because we know that if we change one element in a system there will be consequential changes in the rest.

In an interpersonal relationship, if we are prepared to make a change in our own behaviour, it will induce a change, often quite unconsciously, in the behaviour of the other person. The first change which is made in our behaviour has a particular purpose. We set out to try to align ourselves with the behaviour pattern of the other person. We call establishing this congruent behaviour '**Pacing**' or '**Mirroring**'.

There are many ways in which you can pace another person. You can pace their attitudes, their gestures or body language, their vocabulary, the volume and intonation of their speech.

You can even pace their breathing pattern. Pacing involves presenting, or reflecting back to another person, behaviour patterns in yourself which are most like their own. By your mirroring of what they do, you make it easy for them to feel comfortable. They like people who are like themselves. They are predisposed to agree with people they like.

Establishing rapport by pacing the other person puts you in a position in which you begin to lead. It is important that you know exactly what you are doing and that you remain in control. The pursuit of congruence must not become a limp desire to please. So how do you put it into practice?

If you are confronted with a very angry person and you remain totally passive, you may be in control of yourself, but the probability is that your very passivity may inflame the other person even more. However, if you match their intensity at a slightly lower intensity and combine that with helpful and creative comments, you will notice them calming down quite quickly and you are in a position to be able to lead them into a more amenable mood.

This is not an easy skill to master, but as you work at it you will begin to find more subtle ways to match and mirror rather than simply copying.

You can match the rhythm of someone's fast-paced walk or voice pattern by drumming your fingers on the tabletop. This echo of their behaviour is unstressed but will be picked up by their unconscious mind. If they have been pacing up and down in anger, or because of tension, you can match that pace in the rhythm of your fingers.

Now if you begin to slow the tempo of your own mirroring as

you tap the table, you may find the other person begins to slow the speed of their walk and of course a physiological change can bring about a change of mood.

By matching, mirroring and pacing you have been able to take control and to lead the other person to a more productive state. That new state will be better for them and better for you. The increased rapport will help both of you.

You have to be careful how you pace and mirror certain features of other people, or you can actually destroy rapport rather than create it. This includes things such as strong regional accents, stammering or nervous mannerisms.

If the other person feels that you are imitating things which they do not like about themselves, they will not like what they see reflected back. It will make them feel uncomfortable. Remember, people like people who are like themselves - but that only applies if the reflected likeness is of the things they like about themselves.

Nobody likes to feel that they are being 'sent up' by an unkind imitation.

We have quoted the research which shows that 55% of communication is by our body language. Films made by the Child Development Unit of the Boston University Medical Centre show that, even in the first twelve hours of life, new-born babies are aware of the facial expressions of the adults who surround them. Other films later in life show synchronicity between people in the art of communication.

In his book 'Beyond Culture' Edward T Hall comments on the films -

> *'taken in a variety of settings and circumstances, (they) reveal that when two people talk to each other their movements are synchronised.'*

If you want to check on this for yourself, watch two people having a conversation. When one folds his arms, the other will soon do the same. If one scratches his head, the other follows suit. One pulls at his ear; watch the other. It becomes a ritualised dance. We do it ourselves. It is remarkably difficult to resist!

Talking of dancing, you will know that you cannot dance with another person if your moves are based on conflict! You have to achieve harmony before you can lead the dance - or before you can follow the lead. Dancing depends on rapport. Rapport is a form of dancing.

Historically, women, because of their social position, have had to become better dancers, or pacers, than men. They have had to learn to get what they want by means that are more indirect and more subtle than the overt power-plays of men. This has not encouraged men to find elegant ways of resolving differences. War is the least elegant style of negotiation, and war is a traditional male activity.

Men are more likely to feel that they may be losing their individuality when they pace someone else's behaviour. However, the times are changing and there is no reason why men in general should not become as skilful as women in the art of rapport.

The simple act of pacing body language can have far-reaching results. In some cases it is the only means we have of communicating.

> The most uncommunicative people of all in our society are autistics. They are people who, for whatever reason, are cut off from others and inhabit an entirely closed system of their own. Autistics live in a world that is almost impenetrable. In 1970, Jane Adler, a dance therapist, successfully broke through the barriers surrounding the closed off world of two autistic children.
>
> A film was made of Adler's progress. It begins with her imitation of the children's unco-ordinated and apparently purposeless movements. It ends with **them** following **her**, alternately prancing, romping and playing around in her dance studio with freedom and direction. It is wonderful proof of the power of pacing and leading.

There would have been no point in Adler beginning by saying to the children '*Now look here you two, this anti-social behaviour won't do at all. You ought to behave like this!*' No, she began by **being just like them**. Once she had gained their trust in this way, she was able to lead them into worlds of different experience.

If Adler could do this with some of the least responsive people in our society, imagine what we ought to be able to accomplish with each other.

This skill is easier to master than some others, because it is a matter of becoming aware and taking control of something we have been doing without conscious effort for all of our lives. It begins with simple awareness and sensitivity. For example, most of us are sensitive enough not to talk too loudly and aggressively to a friend who is suffering from an obvious hangover! Similarly, four o'clock in the morning may not be the best time to contact someone if you are hoping to excite them about some brilliant new idea.

Toning our behaviour up or down, to match the behaviour of the person we are with, is the beginning of the art of mastering body language. If you choose to present yourself to someone in a manner which is at odds with that person's own body language, you will create resistance to whatever message you are trying to get across. This reaction has nothing to do with the content of the message, it is all to do with body language which is failing the basic congruency test.

When you succeed in pacing somebody, you are sending out non-verbal messages. *'I'm like you'* - *'You are safe with me'* - *'You can trust me'*; On the other side of the coin, if your body language, your gestures and the speed of your actions are dramatically different from those of the other person, the unspoken message is *'I am different from you.'* Your message will be treated as different from theirs, even when it may be substantially the same.

A business based on a telephone answering service dramatically increased its subscribers when the art of pacing the intonation and rate of speech of the callers was introduced. Because the only contact with potential clients amounted to one or two calls, each conversation had to count.

So a caller who spoke quickly was answered quickly, and slow speakers were answered more slowly. This one simple change resulted in a 30% increase in the number of subscribers.

You will often hear someone say '*I like so and so... they really speak my language.*' This just underlines the fact that it helps to observe the vocabulary and imagery which people use, and then to mirror their style of phraseology when talking to them. Similarly, it makes sense to avoid using vocabulary which is strange to them.

Pacing volume can also produce effective results. Speaking softly to a softly-spoken person quickly generates an atmosphere of trust. It banishes any fear that may be hidden behind the gentleness. In the same way, matching the volume of a loud person will cause them to treat you with respect. You are making it clear that you are not going to be overpowered or bullied. We already mentioned this when we discussed matching the verbal volume of an angry person and then gradually toning the volume down. This is more likely to be effective than speaking to them gently in the first place.

When you give people a reflection of themselves, and even begin by exaggerating that reflection, you can often cause them to modify their behaviour. That idea moves us naturally from the technique of 'pacing' to the related but different technique of 'leading'. Leading becomes possible through rapport and, when used effectively, can increase its effect without disturbing the other person.

Many of these techniques are codified in the science of Neuro-Linguistic Programming which is based largely on the work of the late Milton Erickson - one of the world's leading hypnotherapists. He told a fasinating story about his young son.

'Three-year-old Robert fell down the back stairs, split his lip, and knocked an upper tooth back into the maxilla. He was bleeding profusely and screaming loudly with pain and fright. His mother and I went to his aid. A single glance at him lying on the ground bleeding, his mouth bleeding profusely and blood spattered on the pavement, revealed that this was an emergency requiring prompt and adequate measures.

No effort was made to pick him up. Instead, as he paused for breath for fresh screaming, I told him simply, sympathetically, quickly and emphatically, "That hurts awful, Robert. That hurts terrible."

Right then, without any doubt, my son knew that I knew what I was talking about. He could agree with me and he knew that I was agreeing completely with him. Therefore he could listen respectfully to me because I had demonstrated that I understood the situation fully. . .

Then I told Robert "And it will keep right on hurting." In this simple statement, I named his own fear,   confirmed his own judgement of the situation, demonstrated my good, intelligent grasp of the entire matter and my entire agreement with him, since right then he could foresee only a lifetime of pain and anguish for himself.'

Erickson goes on to tell how he changed Robert's perception by gradually changing his focus, from the pain to speculating as to how many stitches the wound might need, to a favourable comparison with the stitches needed to mend the cuts of his friends, and to the self-esteem arising from having successfully survived the experience.

In this way Erickson moved the boy's attention from the immediate situation to an envisaged and more empowering future condition. It is a superb example of **leading**, first by **pacing** and then by positively leading the other person's experience. This is the art of positive persuasion. It confirms what the other person feels to be true, and then leads them from this shared position to other more rewarding possibilities.

It is the best way forward because people generally resist messages that do not match up with their own vision of the world. That means that even a well-intentioned attempt to help someone is likely to be doomed if we begin by telling them that we think they are wrong! The key to that is to remember that people do things for their own reasons and not for yours.

Before starting to try 'leading', always test for successful 'pacing'. You can do this at the simple physical level by slightly altering your body language.

Watch to see if the other person, consciously or more usually unconsciously, begins to mirror you. You can also do the same thing at the verbal level by throwing out a suggestion in the direction you want to go and watching the response.

In the world of sales, this is called a 'Trial Close.' Have a look at a couple of examples. The first shows how to pick up on a positive response.

You: *So we've agreed that the problem is that the workforce aren't turning up and that it's costing us money?*

Them: *Yes, that's right. We've got to do something about it before the bottom falls out.*

You: *All right. Well do you think it might be a good idea if we did something radical like hiring people on a self-employed basis so that we would only be paying them for the time they are actually working for us?*

Them: *Maybe. How would that work then?*

Next, see what happens when the response is not positive.

You: *So we've agreed that the problem is that the workforce aren't turning up and that it's costing us money?*

Them: *Yes, that's right. We've got to do something about it before the bottom falls out.*

You: *All right. Well do you think it might be a good idea if we did something radical like hiring people on a self-employed basis so that we would only be paying them for the time they are actually working for us?*

Them: *No! That would only worsen relations with the staff, which is the source of the whole problem anyway.*

You: *Good point. Obviously we need to think this thing through carefully. Do you have any ideas?*

What you have done here is you have gone back to a previously agreed position so that you can stay in agreement and then try a new route forward. Here is a basic flow diagram.

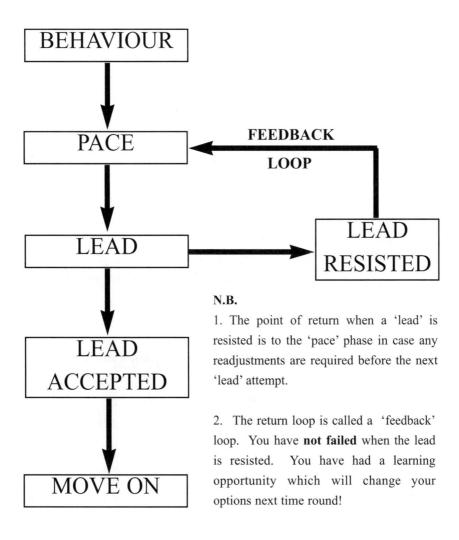

N.B.

1. The point of return when a 'lead' is resisted is to the 'pace' phase in case any readjustments are required before the next 'lead' attempt.

2. The return loop is called a 'feedback' loop. You have **not failed** when the lead is resisted. You have had a learning opportunity which will change your options next time round!

In the course of the last few pages we have quoted, from real life and from sample dialogue, several ways in which language can be used both in pacing and in leading. In each of those cases, everything said was a matter of direct communication; there was no doubt about the meaning of what was being said or about the reason for saying it.

There can be times when words used in a straightforward context can influence the mind of the person who hears them in a quite unexpected way. This can happen quite unintentionally, but if it can be identified and used for deliberate effect, the results can be dramatic. Skilful communicators learn how to use this technique. They find that they can **embed** suggestions or commands into their conversation with other people. If this sounds manipulative in the negative sense, realise that it is only a matter of making deliberate and conscious use of a feature of our language which we use unconsciously and rather clumsily all the time.

Imagine a small child carrying a glass of water across the kitchen floor. Suddenly you shout out *'Be careful! Don't spill the water!'* There are no prizes for guessing what actually happens!

Compare:

'Don't drop that plate!' with *'Carry that plate carefully'*

'Don't use that tone of voice with me!' with
'Please speak nicely to me.'

and

'Don't play in the street where you might get hit by a car' with
'Play in the yard where you will be safe.'

When you look at all those examples you can spot the embedded possibilities.

In each case there is either a negative or a positive command in what has been said. You have probably used all of them yourself at some time. Have you ever consciously spotted what you were doing? If you realised what was happening, would you have chosen the more positive alternative?

If your answer to that last question was 'Yes', you are already prepared to allow yourself to use **embedded commands**, and we do not believe that you would consider that you were being 'manipulative' in any undesirable way! Such commands are effective because they are largely invisible and therefore meet with little resistance, even when they are designed to affect the behaviour of whoever hears them!

Study the following exchange and see how effective the embedded commands could be:

> **Bryan:** *I really don't think that this is the time for me to be spending any more money.*

> **Cheryl:** *Well of course I don't know if this is the time for you to make an investment, but I certainly believe that if you could afford to invest now, you would almost certainly make a lot of money.*

If we return to our suggestion of using techniques parallel to those in Ju-Jitsu or Aikido, we can identify another conversational style in which we use questions at appropriate moments.

People like to talk more than they like to listen. A carefully inserted question can steer someone else's conversation in the direction you want it to go while all the time you are using the other person's flow of verbal energy.

Once again we can listen to Bryan and Cheryl in a series of conversational interludes. You may find yourself admiring Cheryl's methods.

Conversation A

Bryan: *What we need to do, instead of spending all our time operating in this overcrowded market, is to pay more attention to unexplored market areas.*

Cheryl: *That's interesting. Where do you think these areas are?*

Bryan: *Well, I reckon in the South West. We have our team banging away in the North, just like everyone else, when there's this whole untapped area in the South-West.*

Cheryl: *Right. And how do you think we should go into that area?*

Bryan: *Well. . .*

Here, Cheryl is helping Bryan to move his thinking along by prompting him to answer his own questions.

Conversation B

Bryan: *I'm having a lot of trouble getting through to people on the shop floor. They're so busy*

*pushing their own point of view that they
simply won't listen to me. If they did listen,
they might find that I have the answers to
some of their problems.*

Cheryl: *You mean these people are so full of their
own opinions that they can't see that you
have the answer they're looking for because
they just don't listen?*

Bryan: *Yes, that's right, and what's more. . .*

In this case, Cheryl establishes a fair rapport with Bryan by
paraphrasing what he has said originally. Bryan finds it easier to
continue discussion with someone who seems to agree with him.

Conversation C

Bryan: *I'm having a lot of trouble getting through
to people on the shop floor. They're so busy
pushing their own point of view that they
simply won't listen to me. If they did listen,
they might find that I have the answers to
some of their problems!*

Cheryl: *You mean these people are so full of their
own opinions that they can't see that you've
got part of the answer they're looking for.
Whereas if you could* **find some common
ground,** *you might be able to get them to
listen and* **find a solution with them***?*

Bryan: *Yes, that's right, and. . .*

In this final example, Cheryl does the same as in B, but has introduced some embedded commands to suggest a possible solution to Bryan's problem. Because of the rapport, Bryan finds it easy to carry on, without consciously realising what Cheryl has achieved!

As Peak Performers, the first thing we do is to take responsibility for any resistance we may meet, and to recognise it as a result of our own inexpert communication style. **Remember, communication is what is received, not what is intended**. We take the responsibility, not because of 'fault' or 'blame', but because we know that the person who takes responsibility is in position to take control.

To overcome their resistance we begin by removing **our** resistance to **their** resistance. We go with it. We accept it. Where necessary, we are even prepared to **agree** with it.

Even here, the golden rule applies. Find common ground where agreement exists. As always, it will be easier to move from established agreement to further agreement. Certainly it will be easier than trying to move from disagreement to agreement.

Peak Performers do not say '*I just can't understand why you don't want to talk to me! Can't you see that I'm dying to give you the benefit of my expert advice?*' They are much more likely to say '*Yes, I know just how you feel. I quite often don't want to talk to people myself, even if they **really want to help**.*'

A basic rapport has been offered and hopefully it has been accepted. There is a superb embedded command in those last four words. Now that we have established an area of agreement, we stand a much more realistic chance of getting a positive response.

V H F -

T H E   L A T E S T   I N

E F F E C T I V E

C O M M U N I C A T I O N

In the last chapter we told the story of how Milton Erickson dealt with his young son who had had a nasty accident. In the course of his professional life as a hypnotherapist, Erickson had an interesting technique for getting reluctant communicators to open up. He describes it like this:

> *Sometimes I'll ask "What's your name? How old are you? What town do you come from? What baseball team do you support?"*

> *Each time the person struggles to answer and makes the mouth movements to get under way, the next question is asked...You ask a question, just start a pause, and don't give them a chance to respond. With the next question you wait, but not quite long enough. You're so earnest, and it frustrates them until finally they say "Will you shut up? The answer is . . ."!*

Erickson calls this 'building expectancy'. NLP refers to it as 'stacking'. It is an ingenious way to get people to open up. Erickson uses another ploy which is based on seeming to encourage, or give permission to the other person actually to withhold communication. Again we quote his own description.

'Sometimes in the first interview it is necessary to help someone talk. People come to tell you about their problems and yet are reluctant to discuss them. One way to deal with this is to say to them:

"This is your first interview with me. You tell me you want to talk about some very painful things. In other words, I judge there are some things you would rather not tell me. I think you ought not to tell me those things you just can't endure telling me. Tell me the things that you can, with the least amount of pain. Be sure you hold back the things you can't bear to tell me."

The person starts to talk, and at the end of the hour will say, "Well I've told you all the things I just can't bear to tell you!"

What they do is select. They think: "Can I dare tell this or not? I'm free to withhold it, but I guess I'll tell this one."

They always vote in favour of telling. They postpone the telling, but that's what withholding is.'

Erickson's patients communicated with him because they felt they did not have to. There was no sense of coercion. Of course there is also the point that some of us like to do the opposite of what we feel we have been told to do. Incidentally, if you re-read that passage above, did you notice how many times Erickson used the embedded command 'tell me' in his opening words, and this was in a sentence which appeared to give the opposite instruction.

The more you practise these skills, the more fluent you will become in their use, and the more they will become part of your natural pattern. You will discover techniques of your own as you widen your range in response to the Law of Requisite Variety. To develop in this field, you need to sharpen what is called **Sensory Acuity**.

We all live by our five senses, but three in particular - seeing, hearing and feeling - tend to dominate our communication. While we use all our senses, each of us has a preferred sensory style. Some of us are visualisers, thinking largely in pictures. Some of us are auditory; we like to use words to express things wherever we can. Some of us can be described as kinaesthetic; we live in a tactile world in which we like to use our feeling capability.

As a useful shorthand we can describe the three types as **VHF.**

	V H F
V	**Visualising**
H	**Hearing**
F	**Feeling**

Someone who has the necessary sharpened sensory acuity can and should try to identify which of the three categories describes a person with whom they are trying to communicate.

Visualisers think in pictures; they tend to talk rapidly to get all the information that they 'see' across; they use quick gestures.

Auditory hearing types focus on words and since their choice of words is more careful, they tend to speak more slowly in considered manner; they make more economical gestures.

Kinaesthetics tend to 'feel every thing through' very thoroughly; their whole physiological style will be slower and deeper.

Of course these are generalisations, but they have to be to make the concepts clear. Obviously people are a lot more complex than this, not least because none of us is entirely and only V, H or F. We use all our senses to some degree in our verbal communications. What we are talking about is emphasis. At the same time you can imagine that there can be problems and scope for miscommunications between people who are dominantly visualisers and those who are kinaesthetic.

All these ideas are connected with the search for rapport. If you can identify the other person's VHF inclination, you can try to use that style to make communication more simple and effective. How do you do this? **Listen to the way they talk!**

If Mary says that she 'grasps the idea' she may be kinaesthetic. If her future 'looks hazy' she may be a visualiser. If she says 'that rings a bell', she is probably in auditory mood. She may decide to 'look into it' (V) or to 'sound this out' (H) or perhaps to 'explore the issue' (F).

Spotting these trends can be crucial, not least because you cannot **not** communicate. You are always sending out signals whether you realise it or not. The wrong sensory style will create barriers. If you talk loudly and rapidly, attempting to get a lot of eye contact, when you are with a rather shy person who speaks quietly and slowly, what kind of messages do you think that person is going to pick up? How likely are they to be the same as those you believe you are sending out?

On this basis you could understand why, for example, a woman who has a tendency to be auditory ('*You never tell me that you love me*') is liable to be unimpressed by a visually inclined man who always gives her flowers ('*But I'm always **showing** you how much I love you*'). You could understand his frustration as well! It is altogether more effective to notice and to echo the

physiology and language style of the other person. We call it **Matching and Mirroring**. It needs practice. For example, it is sometimes too easy to misinterpret someone's tiredness as boredom. After all, the symptoms can look alike. Then, if you try to stimulate them from what you see as their boredom, their tired reaction to your enthusiasm can be counterproductive.

Communicating with others is obviously more indirect than communicating with yourself. Trial and error is necessary. Working out someone else's VHF preference can offer a tremendous short-cut. You can help yourself in learning how to do it from the cases of some well-known public figures - even though you may never have to communicate with them.

Astronomer Patrick Moore and David Bellamy are both classic examples of the visualiser. Their rapid speech and animated gestures are absolutely typical. Visualisers have to work fast to keep up with the speed of the information they 'see' with their mind's eye.

John Major is a typical auditory. He has the standard mid-tempo exactitude and subdued body language. Soul singer Barry White is a typical kinaesthetic, as his slow, thoroughly sensual savouring of every word and gesture reveal it.

Of course we need to be careful not to oversimplify the situation. As we said earlier, we use all our senses. Our preferences of style are very much context driven. We are governed by the situations we find ourselves in.

The particular examples we chose have highly developed preferences and styles. On occasion they can easily add elements of other styles when they feel they are needed. Some of the greatest communicators would fire on all channels at once.

Who were the great communicators?

Martin Luther King spoke with passion. John F Kennedy spoke with conviction. Adolf Hitler - though you may not consider him admirable - spoke with an almost irresistible fire. They were all people who knew how to behave and sound attractive to their audiences, how to arouse their feelings. This ability to use all the skills and all the styles so as to appeal to the greatest number of other people offers a great advantage. It is part of the reason why Tony Blair, for example, inspires more popularity than John Major.

If we go back to the story of Walt Disney using his three point strategy, at first, as the artist, he would have been dominantly in the Visual mode - not least because he was creating a film, a visual medium. However, in the second stage, as the realist, he would have been in a kinaesthetically-led Feeling mode as he concentrated on how things might be done, on activities. Finally, in the third stage, as the critic, Disney would have been mainly auditory, Hearing the internal dialogue as he used the words, our most precise analytical tool. Certainly all three elements would have overlapped but the three-part multi-sensory appraisal undoubtedly benefited his projects.

Observing the VHF of our friends is a great way to help them and us in our communication with each other. This is the proper application of rapport. You can only lead yourself and others onto higher ground if your intentions are good.

You have to be trustworthy to be trusted.

As you build rapport, mutual trust will grow. If you succeed in mirroring and matching what someone else does, you begin to know what it is like to be that person. Remember, people like people who are like themselves.

Mirroring and matching are an extension of the technique of modelling but with a different purpose. In modelling, we imitate to get the kind of results the other person achieves. In mirroring and matching, we imitate the other person so that we can become more like each other, in the belief that together we will achieve more than either of us could hope to achieve on our own.

Successful communication with others will produce better results than communicating with ourselves alone. When we combine the two together we can exceed our early expectations. That is why the situation is so truly creative.

All this is building rapport. Rapport is a dynamic, spontaneous, moment-to-moment activity. Sometimes we may feel that it already exists in a relationship. One thing, however, is certain. It can be built on and improved by the conscious application of technique.

To underline what we have been saying we will consider a few examples of real life conversations and make some comments about them.

Salesperson: *Have you had a chance to look at my proposal?*

Client: *Yes I have, and I don't feel it meets with our requirements.*

Salesperson: *OK. What parts of it don't look right to you? Maybe I could show more examples that will illustrate more clearly all the benefits of our products.*

Client: *Maybe. I'm not sure. I don't feel that there's any point because I'm not that comfortable about the pricing structure.*

Salesperson: *Have you seen our latest pricing structure document? Because it*

> *paints a bigger picture of what's*
> *possible.*

Client: *Yes, I have.*

Salesperson: *What is it about it that you don't like*
the look of?

It is fairly obvious what is going on here. No rapport leading to
no result on either side. Neither person is aware of the other's
natural style, their VHF. So check to make sure that you are
aware of all the important signs. Read the scene again and notice
all the sensory words used in the conversation. Can you
establish the VHF preference of each of the characters? How
did you get on? Here is the same conversation, only this time
every sensory based word has been typed in **bold letters** or ***bold***
italics.

Salesperson: *Have you had a chance to **look** over*
my proposal?

Client: *Yes I have, and I don't **feel** it meets*
with our requirements.

Salesperson: *OK. What parts of it don't **look***
*right to you? Maybe I could **show***
*more examples that will **illustrate***
*more **clearly** the benefits of our*
products.

Client: *Maybe. I'm not sure. I don't **feel***
that there's any point because I'm
*not that **comfortable** about the*
*pricing **structure.***

Salesperson:	*Have you **seen** our latest pricing structure document? Because it **paints** a bigger **picture** of what's possible.*
Client:	*Yes, I have.*
Salesperson:	*What is it about it that you don't like the **look** of?*

For the sake of clarity we have chosen an obvious example. The words in bold type - **'feel'**, **'comfortable'** and **'structure'** - are all feeling kinaesthetic words. Those in bold italic type - *'look'*, *'show'*, *'illustrate'*, *'clearly'*, *'seen'*, *'paint'* and *'picture'* - are all visual.

All these words clearly type the two speakers. As they are both evidently extreme examples of the types, the conversation is not going well. Neither is aware of the other's style and there is a mutual failure to notice this or to react. Remember, we are limited by what we do not notice. If we wish to build a bridge over differences and establish rapport, we have to be equipped to notice what may be getting in the way. If you can't notice it, you can't fix it!

In the next example, two people, Jenny and Andy, from the same company, are discussing the making of a video about rapport with John who is a film-maker.

John:	*So, tell me, what is the outcome you hope for from this video? Talk me through it, Jenny?*

Jenny: *Well, I see this as an opportunity to illustrate the importance of rapport skills in business today. I believe we need to show the viewer how much of a difference it can make.*

Andy: *Well - er - is that right? Feels a bit woolly and airy-fairy to me. I feel that what people really need is a solid grounding in the skills.*

John: (to Jenny) *When you say 'important', what kind of things sound important to you? What precisely does the viewer need to hear?*

Jenny: *I'm looking for the viewer to see clearly some demonstrations of this skill. Let me* **see** (pauses for a moment and looks up*) I kind of envisage a scene involving people in a typical sales presentation in which clearly there is miscommunication and therefore misunderstanding due to lack of rapport.*

Andy: *Oh I think you're going off at the wrong tangent. I'd feel more comfortable with something that was based on a series of interactive challenges, so that they got a firm grasp on how rapport would work for them. I mean you can show them all you want, but unless you get them doing things they're not going to get a feeling for how it works.*

John: *Well, let's come back and discuss that issue later. Explain to me the overall style you think it needs to make sure it really clicks with the audience.*

Andy: *Well* (pauses for reflection) ...

Jenny: (interrupting) *Well I picture it as being very...*

Andy: *Hang on a minute! Just let me think! You're becoming a real pain in the neck.*

Jenny: (to John) *Here we go again! Sorry about that. Andy and I never seem to see eye to eye on these kinds of things.*

Andy: *It needs to have impact and deliver the message with a punch but without ramming it down their throats. It needs to be paced so that people can understand it - not too fast.*

Jenny: *What? You want to send people to sleep? Is that the idea? It's got to be alive, it's got to be colourful, bright, with lots of action. Fast on the eye. Lots of imagery.*

John: (slightly exasperated) *Well I'm getting a bit confused here! At first I thought we were all in tune, but we don't seem to be singing off the same hymn sheet at all. So listen, tell me again . . .*

Now with your knowledge of VHF and matching other people's styles you can see how rapport is being lost here. So to end this on a happier note, imagine that John the film maker who is an auditory (**H**earing) type has been on an intensive one-day course on 'Rapport'. See what difference he can make as he finds himself in a situation where he is trying to negotiate between **V**isualiser Jenny and kinaesthetic **F**eeler Andy.

John: *So tell me, what is the outcome you hope for from this video? Talk me through it. Jenny?*

Jenny: *Well I see this as an opportunity to illustrate the importance of rapport skills in business today. I believe we need to show the viewer how much of a difference it can make.*

Andy: *Well - er - is that right? Feels a bit woolly and airy-fairy to me. I feel what people really need is a solid grounding in the skills.*

John: (to Jenny) *Help me to get some greater understanding here. If you could throw some light on what you see as being important, and* (to Andy) *if you could help get a grasp on exactly where you're coming from when you speak of 'solid grounding'.*

Jenny: *I'm looking for the viewer to see clearly some demonstrations of this skill. Let me see* (pauses for a moment and looks up) *I kind of envisage a scene involving people in a typical sales presentation in which clearly there is miscommunication and therefore misunderstanding due to lack of rapport.*

Andy: *Oh I think you're going off at the wrong tangent - I'd feel more comfortable with something that was based on a series of interactive challenges, so that they got a firm grasp on how rapport would work for them. I mean you can show them all you want but unless you get them doing things they're not going to get a real feeling for how it works.*

John: (to Andy) *Ah! So what Jenny is getting at is that she wants the viewer to get a handle on the issue through witnessing a concrete example of people getting stuck in miscommunication because they lack the knowledge and understanding of rapport skills -* (to Jenny) *And I think what Andy means is that he wants to see the importance of rapport highlighted through illustrating how this material actually works. Is that it?*

Jenny: *Yes. That's close. Maybe we're not poles apart after all!*

Andy: *Yes. I think we're definitely on track.*

It is interesting to see how quickly they were able to reach agreement. Once John had become aware of the issue, he was able to mirror the sensory language styles of both people and translate the one to the other. The result was congruency - and since people like people who are like themselves, they find it easy to agree with people they like.

Being or becoming like other people involves a lot of matching and mirroring. It is something we all do. We just need to make it conscious. Awareness changes everything.

The true benefit of these skills which are so valuable to Peak Performers will only become apparent when they become a natural part of your communication style. We have said it takes practice. But realise that opportunity for practice occurs every time you communicate - the opportunity surrounds us every day!

We need to raise our awareness and become keen observers of how people interact with each other. Then we need to develop the flexibility to match our style to theirs. Once we have done that, we are ready to move up a gear. Our communication will become truly creative.

We will be creating Rapport.

BREAKTHROUGH
TO
PEAK PERFORMANCE

Part Five

CREATIVE
COMMUNICATION

PRECISION, HAND IN HAND WITH CLARITY

'He who is not busy being born is busy dying.'

When the poet said that, he was creating a metaphor about psychological growth or decay, highlighting the essentially dynamic nature of life. This dynamism is particularly apparent in our acts of communication. When we communicate, we either get closer or we create barriers which make us drift further apart. Whoever we are, whether we are trying to persuade, influence, sell, exchange ideas or merely make an enquiry, the resulting communication process will either bring us nearer to our goal or further away from it. We cannot be static.

Today's technology allows us to surf the information network and many of us find that absorbing, fascinating and rewarding. However we should realise that in our daily lives we continue having to surf the **inter-personal** network. We have to be able to communicate with people and our success in reaching our goals will reflect the development of our communications skills. We live in a social system in which we have to work together in an increasingly interdependent way and that underlines the importance of those skills.

In the achievement of our goals, one of our greatest resources is each other. Access to that resource depends on excellent communication. Excellence involves accuracy in understanding others and in the way we express ourselves. Excellence is about being precise and that means gaining mastery of the whole communication process.

In the last chapter of Part Four we dealt with the whole question of reading the non-verbal body language and attitude signals of other people and also how to classify their verbal styles. The pursuit of excellence in communication stresses the importance of being aware of the structure and use of language. Above all, if we are determined to achieve the highest standard, we must be prepared to develop our listening skills.

Perhaps more than any of the others we have considered, listening skills need constant practice before they become an automatic part of our personal style of behaviour. It is well worth while spending the necessary time and energy establishing these good habits; a high degree of our success depends on them.

Make no mistake about it, we are talking about success of a high order here. This is all about synergy. This is about one plus one making three! It is about the amazing results we can achieve when we work effectively together. It is about realising that when two people work together in harmony their combined achievements are going to be much greater than the sum of what they might have achieved working as two separate individuals.

Communication skills, fully developed and mastered, provide you with a power tool. You need to take care how you use it. A knife can inflict great damage, but in the hands of a surgeon it can heal. We should follow the surgeon's example and be creative in the use of the power tool we have. The first step is to take responsibility for the process.

Every area of Peak Performance involves taking responsibility.

It was true for our motivation. It was true for our beliefs. It is true for communication which gives us so much power, as we are able to release the full potential within ourselves and between ourselves and others.

In Part Four we learnt how to establish rapport. The question is, what are we going to do with it now that we have got it? Are we just going to hang around enjoying each other's company, or are we going to use the communication process to take us to the place where we achieve powerful results?

When we decide to make that forward move, we must have established a win/win relationship with the other person. Both parties must benefit. Win/lose outcomes, in which one person exploits the other, have no place in creative communication. It is obvious that they can only be destructive. Notice that the destructive result does not only apply to the exploited person, it applies to whoever is doing the exploiting as well. You get what you give.

> *'In the end the love you take*
> *Is equal to the love you make.'*

For love you can substitute any other element of personal relationship. The law of karma or balancing of consequences is as fundamental as the laws of gravity.

Only win/win relationships are ultimately worthwhile because they release the potential in both of us. They create positive outcomes which continue to ensure further success. These win/win relationships are the outcome of successful communication and mutual understanding.

How do we achieve this?

We begin by establishing rapport and then we must concentrate on the content and value of what we are communicating. What are we transmitting and receiving in our mutual exchanges? The answer is descriptions of our experiences, and, to describe those experiences, we need to use words. Therefore we need to underline the importance of words themselves.

You may well be thinking that we have said earlier that words only convey 7% of communication. That is still true. You do not have to understand every word to pick up a lot of the message. Turn on the radio and if you tune it at random you will soon find a station broadcasting in a foreign language. Even though you may not understand the words, you will be able to judge the emotions of the speakers. That is why we can often enjoy songs being sung in a language we cannot speak.

Though the meaning of the words may only convey 7% of the message, it is the crucial 7% on which the rest depends. It is like the missile heads of the weapons in a nuclear submarine - quite small in relation to the whole machine, but vital to its task and purpose.

It is the same with language. Words have impact. Language is the most awesome and sophisticated tool ever developed by the human race. Precisely because it is so rich, it is full of multiple meanings and ambiguities which can confuse the message it is meant to convey. Almost by its very nature it can be full of hidden meanings either accidentally or intentionally.

Think of the signs you can see on the London Underground which say '*Dogs must be carried on the escalator.*' Does this mean I have to find a dog to carry before I can use the escalator?

Then there is the probably apocryphal case of the advertisement *'Wanted. Wooden stool for milkmaid with three legs.'*

Use of simple logic makes both these examples easy to clarify, but that is not always the case. At the same time, since language is our primary means of communication, we need to make what we say as clear and unambiguous as possible. Look at it in this way. In the first place we have an experience, then we represent it in language. There is a gap between the experience and our verbal expression which arises from it. In that gap many things can happen!

We are inclined to generalise from our experience. For example, if the first teacher you ever met was unpleasant, you might go on to believe and therefore represent all teachers as unpleasant. If your first client or your first customer was difficult and awkward to deal with, you might be tempted to generalise once again in the same way, distorting your future business relationships.

Anthony Robbins, who featured earlier in this book when we told the story of his challenge to the American Army, refers to the use of biased, or generalised or unspecific language as being '*fluffy*'. He has identified the need to be able to recognise the fluff in our communications and to learn the art of clarification or '**Fluff-Busting**'.

Without that skill, our tendency to generalise can easily take us away off track in our dealings with each other. For instance, consider the following conversation. Does it have a familiar ring to it?

> **Walter:** *All your people are really unhelpful and rude.*
>
> **Sophie:** *No they aren't.*
>
> **Walter:** *Yes they are - and they're never there when I need them.*
>
> **Sophie:** *What do you mean they're never there? When aren't they there?*
>
> **Walter:** *Whenever I need them. They're never there. Every time I come round to ask about something.*
>
> **Sophie:** *Don't be stupid!*
>
> **Walter:** *Who are you calling stupid?*
>
> **Sophie:** *Well I know for a fact that they **must** be there.*

Walter: *Well you obviously don't know anything about what really goes on around here.*

Sophie: *I bet I know more than you do.*

Walter: *Oh come on! - Now you're being stupid.*

Sophie: *No I'm not.*

Walter: *Anyway, what's that got to do with it? We're here to talk about how unhelpful your staff are, not how stupid we are! Which **I'm** not by the way.*

Sophie: *Well if you weren't, we wouldn't have to have all this rubbish about my people being unhelpful, would we? They've got a reputation for being very helpful, really.*

Walter: *That's not what I've heard!*

Sophie: *Well you obviously don't talk to the right people then, do you?*

Walter: *Anyway it's obviously true, because you haven't been much help yourself!*

Have you ever heard that kind of conversation? Be honest! Have you ever taken part in that kind of exchange yourself? That soap opera conversational style runs like an epidemic through much of our communications because we not only have little control of our state, we also often have inadequate control over our language.

To help with this challenge, we want to introduce you to something called **The Precision Model**.

The left hand which we call the Recognition Hand contains our most typical generalisations and language distortions. The right hand is called the Questioning Hand and is designed to help clarify and 'fluff-bust' the distortions. Each finger of the left hand in turn supplies an example of the violations which we can allow to slip into our language and the matching finger on the right hand has the appropriate response.

Exercise 24 'Touch Typing'

You can learn them and commit them to memory by tapping the fingers together until what they represent is firmly wired into your internal mental circuitry. The point about the Precision Model or the fluff-buster is that it is designed to help in three particular ways;

1. To help us to say what we mean as **precisely** as possible.
2. To help us to understand as **clearly** as possible what other people mean.
3. To help those other people to understand **exactly** what they really **do** mean.

Take the fingers in turn and run through the model beginning with the little fingers of both hands.

On the Recognition hand we have 'Always', 'Every' and 'Never'. These words create big generalisations, and, when they are used, the best response is 'Really?' together with a repeat of the generalisation.

'You always say that!' replied to with **'Really? Always?'**

Moving along to the next finger on the Recognition hand we find 'Should', 'Shouldn't', 'Must' and 'Can't'. The response on the corresponding finger reads 'What would happen if...?' or a similar question.

'I can't possibly do that!' responded to with **'What would happen if you did?'** or perhaps **'What's preventing you?'** These replies open up possibilities in the other person's mind and can create a new awareness.

The middle finger carries the one word 'Verbs'. The clarifying response is simply 'How?'

'Those people are really unhelpful!' Response: 'How, specifically are they unhelpful?' The plan here is to bring about focus and move the use of the word nearer to clarification.

The index finger shows 'Nouns' as the generalisation and 'Who?' or 'What?' as the response. We can use another element of the same example as before.

'Those people are really unhelpful!' Response: 'Who, exactly, is being unhelpful?'

Finally, on the thumb, there are the comparison words 'Best', 'Better', 'Worst' and 'Too' with the reply 'Compared to what?' For example, if you like to think to yourself 'I'm too sexy for this book!' the reply might be 'Really? Too sexy compared to whom?' We will not be insulted if you choose to reply 'Well, to you the authors and editor for a start!'

Perhaps we can see what happens to Walter and Sophie if one of them applies these principles and uses the Precision Model in their conversation.

> **Walter:** *All your people are really unhelpful and rude!*
>
> **Sophie:** *Really? I'm surprised to hear that. Unhelpful and rude? What, all of them?*
>
> **Walter:** *Well, all right, maybe not **all** of them.*
>
> **Sophie:** *Who specifically do you have in mind when you say that, then?*
>
> **Walter:** *I'm thinking of John Smith for a start.*

Sophie: *What? John Smith unhelpful and rude? Surely not? How specifically is he unhelpful and rude?*

Walter: *He doesn't listen to my point of view and is very abrupt with me.*

Sophie: *I will speak to John about this specific point. What about the rest of the team? How do you find them?*

Walter: *Oh, they're quite pleasant and eager to help.*

This is quite a change from the earlier conversation. In this case the issue is gradually coming more into focus and moving closer to a position where a solution can be found. Sophie has made ideal use of the Precision Model. It is designed for use in situations where vagueness and unhelpful generalisations are obscuring the issues and making resolution difficult.

It is important to realise that this technique of using the Precision Model is not designed for every situation and every conversation.

There is nothing wrong with generalisations as such. Without them, thought itself would become impossible. If you were to say, for example, '*The Universe is too big to get round in a day*' and someone responded by asking '*Compared to what?*' you would be justified in wondering where they came from! Or if someone said to you that all water is wet and you jumped in with '*What, **all** water?*' that person would be quite reasonably justified in thinking you a bit daft!

The Precision Model itself needs to be used with precision.

217

Looking back to the revised conversation between Walter and Sophie we can see how the Precision Model acts as a very effective tool. It takes a huge generalisation and, through a series of questions, makes it increasingly more specific. Applied like this, in the right way and in the right place, you can find that problems between people can become more manageable. Becoming more accurately defined makes a problem or a difficulty much more susceptible to solution.

The main thing is to use the tool to draw out more information. The more you have, the more precise your understanding becomes and the better your communication. One word of warning. Remember the importance of maintaining rapport when you are using the technique. We are not in the business of making people feel that they are under interrogation. That is one good reason for trying to avoid using the question *'Why?'* or *'Why not?'*

When people hear those words they often react by beginning long justifications or by looking for excuses or someone else to blame. They hear the dreaded *'Why?'* and hear it as an accusation. In the same way, direct questions have to be used with some sensitivity. In fact it is often a good idea to use question forms which we call 'softeners' like *'I'm wondering how...?'* or *'I'm curious about...'*

Look at two different responses to the statement *'I'm going to improve my performance.'*

First *'How, specifically?'* and secondly *'That's interesting. I'm curious to know how, specifically, you're planning to do that.'* There can be little doubt as to which of the two responses is the more likely to give real encouragement and draw out more meaningful further information.

When people use generalisations, they very often tend to be negative. We have already discussed why this happens. Continuing from the idea of avoiding *'Why?'* because of its potential for negative reaction, we want to concentrate on any other ways of avoiding negative trends. We believe that the other little word *'but'* (and its very close relation *'however'*) should also be avoided in constructive conversation. Of course both words have a perfectly justifiable place in the language, but (!) they often introduce negative reactions in communication.

When someone is putting forward an idea and hears a reply which begins *'I hear what you're saying, but...'* or *'I see what you mean, however...'*, they are likely to feel that they are being devalued. They sense that their idea is going to be resisted and then they begin to close down the channels of communication as rapport begins to fade away.

Luckily there is a useful alternative when it comes to managing difficulties. The potentially negative word *'but'* can often be replaced in what you say by the wonderfully effective and equally simple word *'and'*. This little word establishes an agreement frame in a dialogue which allows us to put an opposite point of view to someone without creating resistance.

Once again compare these two responses which might be used in a common situation, in conversation with someone who has just said that meetings are a waste of time.

1. *'I understand what you mean about the new marketing material, but it won't work with that strapline.'*
2. *'I understand what you mean about the new marketing material and I think we could look at some alternative strap lines to the ones suggested!'*

The first response is unlikely to change the other person's mind. There is clearly insufficient rapport between you. On the other hand, the second response uses the word '*and*' in the skilful pursuit of continuing rapport. The most likely and desirable consequence is that at least the other person will listen to the reasoning behind what you have to say.

L I S T E N   V E R Y

C A R E F U L L Y

In communication you are only limited by the amount you can notice. We can only notice by listening and observing. Each is a skill which can be improved by practice and application.

In discussing rapport, we have already examined the skills of observation in some detail.

Now we will consider the skill of listening, because we need to learn to listen so that we can listen to learn.

This is particularly important when you realise that we are taught reading, writing and talking, whereas most people do not understand that listening is a skill quite separate from the physical act of hearing.

Listening is the fourth channel of effective communication.

We can all benefit from practising to improve the skill. Once they begin to practise, most people are surprised to discover that listening is a very proactive business.

Stephen Covey, some of whose ideas we have mentioned earlier, devised a five-level structure for listening methods. Within that structure we have several choices in any conversation.

1. We can ignore what the other person is saying.
2. We can pretend to listen, while remaining pre-occupied with other things.
3. We can select what we listen to, hearing only what we want to hear.
4. We can actually pay attention to the other person.
5. We can show and create empathy as we listen.

We want to focus on this fifth concept of empathic listening. In this style, which is best of all, we reflect back what is being communicated. We work from the other person's map, from their model of the world. We do not try to impose our own frame of reference.

We will communicate most effectively if we operate from the other person's map and avoid imposing our own. If we are not aware of this, we often **presume** many things about the other person. We find ourselves in effect mind-reading, quite often without being conscious of the fact. This leads on to giving advice or indulging in telling them what **we** think they should do, making that judgement on the basis of our own experience rather than their own.

This is not the most helpful of communication styles, especially if we are working in a sensitive area.

What we can do is combine listening skills with the fluff-busting techniques of the Precision Model. This will give ourselves a double-barrelled approach to improving our conversation and the effectiveness of our communication.

To get an idea of how these can be applied, we are going to introduce a dialogue between a married couple. We hope that you will be able to identify some familiar attitudes, and, from our comments, be able to work out how to deal with them.

First meet the characters. Mike and Sue have recently moved into a new neighbourhood. This move has coincided with a change in Mike's business responsibilities, meaning that he has to spend more time away from home. This has brought good financial news but it means Sue has less of Mike's support. She finds herself faced with a real challenge because they have two young children who have had to start at new schools.

Mike has heard that one of the kids is having trouble with his teachers, and the other is missing her old friends. As a result, their behaviour at home is becoming difficult and unsettled.

It is two weeks since he was last able to get home and things may have changed. He is concerned about the situation and wants to help. He is just passing through between business trips and he grabs the opportunity to speak to Sue when she gets home from dropping the children off at school.

Note A

Mike: *Oh, hi Sue. I've been meaning to talk to you for a while because I can see that you're really struggling at the moment, aren't you?* (he doesn't wait for an answer) *Why don't you tell me about the problem?*

Sue: (slightly taken aback, on the defensive) *Well, I wouldn't say I'm struggling exactly. It's all the changes they keep making. It seems to me that the problems are being* *made by other people. It's nothing to do with me. Things are too complicated.*

Note B

Mike: *But I think the problem is really your attitude, Sue. After all, Joan always got things sorted out when she and Alan moved out here and she's in the same situation as you, isn't she?*

Sue: *Yes, but that's Joan, not me. I can't do things like her. Anyway she's been here longer than I have.*

Note C

Mike: *The thing is Sue, why don't you think it was right for us to come here any more? Your heart's not really in it, is it?* (again he does not wait for an answer) *Why don't you try thinking about things in a different way and try changing your attitude?*

Note D

Sue: *But that'll never work! There's nothing wrong with my attitude anyway. It's just that the kids are always giving me the runaround. What I think you should do, instead of talking to me, is to talk to them about what they need to do.*

Mike: *Well, you're right up to a point, Sue, certainly, but that fact shouldn't affect you to the degree that it has. It can only be your attitude*

Sue: (not listening) *I mean, they're never there when I need them to be, and even when they are there, they never listen to what I'm saying.*

Mike: (not listening either) *Three months ago, when we first moved in, I remember thinking how brilliantly you were dealing with the whole situation, and I thought that you really believed we were doing the right thing, but I don't think you still do!*

Sue: (getting annoyed) *Yes, but I think you're missing the whole point and I want to know what you're going to do to sort out the problem.*

Mike: (also annoyed) *Well I need to know what you're going to do to improve your attitude!*

Sue: *But I just can't improve my attitude under these circumstances.*

Mike: *Why not?*

Sue: *Well, like I said, but I don't think you've been listening, there's all the changes the kids are going through, change after change after change - almost for the sake of it - at least, that's how it feels sometimes - and the teachers aren't doing their job properly - and on top of that, you're never around to help out any more....*

That seems like a good place to stop before Sue and Mike get into a full scale row! Obviously these two people are steering themselves straight into a lose/lose situation.

During that conversation, which happened to be between a husband and wife, many of the communication failures that happen in everyday life were illustrated. Whether we are in our own roles as employers, employees, parents, children, business associates or even friends, we tend to repeat the same patterns in our communications. Whatever your particular vocation or personal situation, you were probably able to identify in that conversation a number of violations of the strategies we have discussed.

It might be a good idea if we review the conversation together to spot the violations. We might be able to re-script the exchange and produce a successful outcome for Mike and Sue.

Mike's first three contributions do not exactly help in getting things off to a positive start.

At **A**, he has already assumed that Sue's behaviour indicates that she is in difficulties. **He** has evaluated the situation as needing talking through. He has presumed that the situation adds up to a '**problem**' for Sue and that word carries on through the talk.

At **B**, he assumes that Sue's attitude is the source of 'the problem'. He does not bother to ask questions to find out if that is true, he **tells** Sue that it is the case. It may be so, on the other hand it may be wide off the mark.

Also at **B**, Mike's reference to and comparison with Joan is not the most sensitive approach. He is so wrapped up in his own viewpoint that he is busily lowering Sue's emotional situation.

At **C**, Mike says: *The thing is Sue,* **why don't you think it was right** *to come here any more? Your heart's not really in it, is it? Why don't you try thinking about things in a different way and* **try changing your attitude?**

This is a classic disaster speech! There are three presumptions in it plus an example of 'telling' in just three sentences. No wonder they go on to get into trouble!

You can see, from what we have already pointed out, just how dangerous presumptions can be. They are the mark of a lazy communicator.

For instance, say you work in Sales and a customer tells you that they want good service. If you presume that you know what they mean by 'good service', without bothering to find out exactly what it implies, you may be well on the way to losing a potentially good customer.

Just think about that for a moment. Even as you read what we have said, you might be thinking that you understand 'good service' already.

Do you? Are you absolutely certain? Think for a moment.

For one customer, it might mean special discounts.

For another, it might be a matter of always delivering on schedule.

For another, it might be a matter of providing a better alternative product if it becomes available.

For another, it might mean always checking back to see if there are going to be any changes.

For another, it might mean good after-sales care and attention!

Perhaps 'good service' was not quite as simple a concept as you thought!

Returning to Mike and Sue, in the exchanges after **D** we can see that their level of listening is changing. They have moved to Level 2 of our original list.

They are concentrating on their next contribution more than on what is being said. As things go on, they get worse as the two of them move down a level to where they are hardly even pretending to listen.

Throughout the whole conversation they have consistently violated the rules for constructive communication. This has not only come as a result of presumptions and failing to listen to each other; in addition, many of their expressions are full of words and phrases which are ripe for the fluff-busting ideas.

Just look at Mike's first statements. It includes *'you're struggling'* - an unspecified verb, and *'the problem'* - an unspecified noun. In his next remark he produces *'attitude'* - again an unspecified noun and then goes on to say that *'Joan always'* - a classic generalisation.

Sue does not do much better. She speaks of *'the changes **they** make'* - an unspecified noun, *'problems are being **made**'* - an unspecified verb, *'**things are too complicated**'* - a comparison, and later *'I **can't do** things'* - setting rules.

Exercise 25   Fluff-Bust
You can set yourself the exercise of going through the whole
exchange to spot the numerous other examples.

There are more examples, but already we have identified enough
to show that Mike and Sue could have got off to a better start in
terms of mutual understanding from the very beginning. That in
turn would have created more trust. Remember too that trust can
be undermined by the misuse of that little word 'but'. There were
two particular examples of just such a mistake.

> **Sue:**   *Yes, **but** that's Joan not me.*
> and
> **Mike:**   *Well, you're right up to a point, Sue,*
> *certainly **but** that fact shouldn't affect you to*
> *the degree that it has.*

As we have said before, it is better to work from agreement to
agreement than to try to get from disagreement to agreement.

Finally in our analysis of the ill-fated conversation we come to
the 'Why?' question, or in this case 'Why not?' Right at the end
of the exchange when Sue says '*I can't*', Mike's response is '*Why
not?*' That produces a stream of self-justification and transferred
blame, because Sue understandably interprets it as an accusation
rather than as a sympathetic empathic enquiry.

After all that analysis, the time has come to see if we can come
up with a more constructive script for Mike and Sue than the
original.

> **Mike:**   *Oh, hi Sue! Have you got a moment or two?*
> *I've been wanting to talk to you about how*
> *things are going.*

Sue: *Yes, sure. No problem! Well, actually that's not quite true. I do have one or two problems at the moment and I'm glad that you're around right now, because I wouldn't mind talking them over.*

Mike: *Fine. OK. So you feel as though you've still got a few problems?*

Sue: *Well, yes. For one thing I find the kids are being really difficult. They don't seem to be there when I need them and even when they are there, they don't seem to listen!*

Mike: *I can see it's making you feel pretty frustrated.*

Sue: *Yes I am. And it's beginning to get me down.*

Mike: *What exactly is it that it's doing to you? How does it affect you?*

Sue: *Well I think it's starting to affect everything I do.*

Mike: *In what way exactly?*

Sue: *Well everything just gets me down. Things are just at their worst.*

Mike: *Really at their worst? Compared to any other times?*

Sue: *Well, certainly compared to a month ago.*

Mike: (after a slight pause to allow him to 'lead' into a change of direction) *By the way, have you seen much of Joan lately?*

Sue: *No I haven't. Why? Do you think she could help?*

Mike: *I'm not really sure. What do you think?*

Sue: *Maybe she could. She has been here longer than us and she must have been in similar situations herself.*

Mike: *Well why not look her up? Anyway I'm glad we have this chance to talk all this through properly.* (another pause) *What would you really like?*

Sue: *Well I'd like to be really enthusiastic again. That's obvious. It would make me feel on top form again, particularly if all the other stuff was sorted out as well.*

Mike: *Oh! What other stuff is that?*

Sue: *You know, the teachers in the new school.*

Mike: *What about them? What exactly is it about the teachers?*

Sue: *Well **they** never take the time to find out about the kids.*

chapter 18

Mike: *All of them? Anyone in particular?*

Sue: *It's the Deputy Head. He just doesn't want to know.*

Mike: *What would it do for you if he did?*

Sue: *Life would certainly be a lot easier.*

Mike: *And?*

Sue: *Well, I think I'd get a lot more co-operation from the kids, maybe.*

Mike: *Is there something stopping the Deputy Head being co-operative?*

Sue: *We don't seem to get on. I guess there's a lack of rapport!*

Mike: *And do you think there might be any particular way you could improve things there?*

Sue: *Well, maybe if I . . .*

So there they go. No chance of a major row developing this time.

They are well on the way to a positive solution using the creative communicative skills we have discussed.

There has been empathic listening, fluff-busting using the Precision Model and that little word '*and*' has kept the agreement frame going.

We do not claim to be either a Shakespeare or a Harold Pinter and we have obviously helped our pair of characters, both when they were demonstrating how not to communicate, and also when they manage things more effectively. The reality of the conversation is not the issue.

What is important is the opportunity to study the techniques which we have been discussing - even if only in a pair of fictitious exchanges.

A R E   Y O U
R E C E I V I N G   M E ?

You may have been feeling that some of the second conversation between Mike and Sue in the last chapter was rather stilted. Perhaps that was because of their lack of practice in the art and technique of using improved communication skills! It was only their first attempt.

Simply knowing about the skills is not enough. They have to become like second nature to you and that takes practice, just like riding a bicycle or juggling. Be prepared to put in the time and the stage will come when you use the skills automatically without having consciously to think about it.

The results of your efforts make it all worth while. You will find that you will be able to reach quickly to the heart of an issue and to isolate what are the significant elements. You do this by leading people you may be talking to. You use a series of questions or comments in your conversation, which result in them becoming more and more specific in describing what they know or what they feel.

Other people will find you helpful as long as you concentrate on maintaining your rapport with them and as long as you resist the temptation to become aggressive or impatient. You will find that you begin to think more clearly as you make sure that you fluff-bust your own contributions. You will improve your control over your own feelings which will allow you to understand the feelings of others. You teach yourself not to over-react to the distortions in other people's descriptions. That, of course, may be a polite way of saying that *you should not over-react even when you know they are telling lies!*

There is another area where your training will apply.

There are many places where people deliberately and skilfully misuse and distort language for their own gain. Advertising and politics are the brand leaders with the concepts of Astrology not far behind.

When you hear **'Vote for X and enjoy all the advantages of a prosperous future',** you, with your training, will be able to ask immediately *'Really? All?'* and *'What advantages? Tell me - specifically.'* and *'How prosperous, exactly?'*

You will be able to analyse the advertisers' claims with an equally enquiring approach. Claims of **'Improved'**, **'Better'** or **'Whiter'** will produce the same query - *'Than what?'*.

You may even begin to ask yourself if their previous product maybe was not as good as they claimed! If that is the case, why should you suddenly begin to believe them this time.

When you think about it, you can see the enormous advantages which you will have gained by understanding how to fluff-bust even the most experienced and skilful purveyors of super-fluff.

We have recognised the benefits of listening and the fact that it is a skill which can be improved by training. Listening can be taught. Why then is it so rare? One of the things which often get in the way is our own internal dialogue. There is a constant stream of chatter that runs through our minds and stops us from hearing clearly what other people are saying to us. The volume of this internal talk decides which of the five levels of listening we are on. The lowest level is when our internal talk is so busy that we simply ignore the communications of others.

A consultant tells this story which explains exactly the effect which we are discussing and also how he found a way to deal with it.

'A while ago I had a visitor who was so preoccupied and abstracted in his manner that communication was a real struggle. He had come to talk to me about a problem but I had difficulty finding out what it was. Although we were sitting close together, we might as well have been at the opposite ends of a football stadium. He was unable to pay attention to what I was saying and many of his own sentences went unfinished. Obviously he had a lot on his mind!

The fact was that the volume of traffic in his head was so great that, without him being aware of it, he was losing touch with the outer world. The question I faced was how to make him aware of the situation.

There did not seem to be much to be gained by simply trying to shout at him; that would only have destroyed whatever relationship we might have created.

Then I had a bright idea. I still had my tape recorder with me which I had been using to record various conversations earlier in the day. I put it down on the table between us and turned it on to 'play' at a moderate level which was just enough to be intrusive.

*My visitor noticed **that**.*

I asked him to try to ignore the sounds and to carry on with the conversation. "It might be an interesting way for you to realise how difficult it is for you to hear me and for me to get through to you." I explained. "The noise coming from the tape machine may seem like an obstacle between us, but it's really only an external version of what's going on inside your mind. All that self talk you're doing is preventing us from communicating . . . see what I mean?"

All this time the machine was playing and my visitor looked at me with a puzzled expression on his face. "I'm sorry," he said, "could you say that again? I can't hear a word you've been saying because of that bloody tape player!"

*When I stopped the machine and explained the point
of what I had done, I found that I was able to get his
full attention.'*

The consultant had found the tape player a useful tool in that
situation, but you cannot re-wind conversations in real life.
Because of that, opportunities are missed and errors are made.

It does not take much to allow your attention to wander to some
internal concern which gains a life of its own and grabs your
mind. Then suddenly you realise with a start that the person you
seem to be listening to has said something interesting. You
notice that much with the Level 2 attention you were giving.
Unfortunately it has gone and you have missed it.

The same thing happens with selective listening, when we only
hear whatever supports our own view. Then we can easily miss
something said which is vitally important to the other person.
Our reply becomes totally inappropriate. The other person is
convinced that we must be entirely self-centred and feels driven
away from us. Even while they are talking to us, we are busily
concentrating on our own reply. If that is how we listen, rapport
soon flies out of the window!

Much useful communication can be achieved at Level 4 by
attentive listening but Peak Performers will want to operate in
the best and most effective way. This can be found by empathic
listening at Level 5.

We spoke of this earlier. It is the stage when we can receive
everything being broadcast by the other person 'loud and clear'.
It comes to us in full stereophonic VHF because all our own
VHF channels are open instead of being turned inwards.

In this condition, we do not judge the other person because we are fully engaged with them at the highest level of rapport. We do not probe, we lead and we let things emerge. We do not agree or disagree, we simply reflect. In this state we naturally find ourselves mirroring the other person's language, maintaining eye contact in an unselfconscious manner and being totally present.

This fully engaged and proactive listening is sometimes called '**Listening with the eyes for feeling**'. We do not pre-frame the other person by saying things like *'Wow! You're frowning. You must really be angry,'* even though we may have noticed the fact and have drawn that conclusion. Saying it would be likely to annoy anyone! Remember, making assumptions is a sign of a lazy listener.

In empathic listening there is no room and no need for this kind of mind reading. We are more likely simply to lead so that we can enquire about the frown, in which case we may discover that there is anger behind it. On the other hand, we might find out that the person simply has a headache! In either case, discovering information is what happens at this listening level. At this stage, we are so naturally tuned in that we can often assess the other person's response even before it becomes verbal.

Imagine what it is like to be listened to at this level.

You may wonder how we know when it is happening. It becomes quite obvious. We know we are being really listened to when we are asked a question arising from what we have just said which helps to create more understanding. It is only when we feel listened to that we feel inclined to explore differences of opinion which may exist between us. How does that make both of us feel? We feel valued and that feeling inspires trust. In turn, trust makes many things possible.

One important note of warning is worth sounding. In all this process we should not say farewell to our own critical faculties. While we set out to establish rapport so that we can communicate and establish trust, we cannot afford to allow ourselves to be swept along by a warm tide of the feeling of good-fellowship which rapport can induce, in a direction which we know inside ourselves to be clearly wrong. We have the right to retain a sense of judgement!

So we have reached the emotional and ethical aspects of creative communication.

The fact that so many of us are continually acting out automatic sequences of behaviour patterns can offer a severe challenge to communication. Something in the environment can act as a stimulus which sparks off a routine piece of behaviour which prevents any new understanding for as long as it lasts.

We all know couples who continually re-run the same arguments again and again. It is interesting to note that invariably in these situations both parties blame each other for what is happening. This means that they feel able to place the responsibility for the resulting low state outside of themselves.

Now they can convince (or satisfy) themselves that they have, or feel they have, no power to control it. It is the other person's fault.

You can be sure that there is no true listening going on. In fact, emotional arguments such as these give the best possible examples of how to violate all the positive communication guidelines which we have been describing. There is no rapport. There is no pacing - apart from increasingly negative reaction. There is unlikely to be any VHF connection.

To be honest, we know how easy it is to be swept along in such a situation. Most of us have found ourselves being provoked by our own emotional states into highly charged and destructive pieces of behaviour. We feel compelled to go through certain routines and it is often very difficult to find the handbrake.

We have looked at the phenomena behind this on several occasions. We know that, unless we run our own representations, they will run us. This was true of the mental movies in the earlier chapters. It is true of the self-talk we have just discussed.

When we 'take off' emotionally, we have usually allowed these systems to get out of control, because we have temporarily forgotten that **we** can control **them**. We have been totally unconscious of the fact that we are running on subjective programmes, because we have failed to distinguish them from reality.

These automatic subjective programmes, by their existence, make us poor listeners and therefore poor communicators. There is so much internal traffic in our minds. It is made even worse by the huge quantity of low quality information thrown at us by the media. It all causes a dramatic fall in our powers of observation.

Have you ever been driving on a long car journey and reached to turn on the radio - only to find that it is already on? It is actually quite a common occurrence. T S Eliot describes it thus. *'Distracted from distraction by distraction.'*

A Zen student spent years studying and meditating. He finally went to visit the Zen Master to see if he could pass the test and be admitted to the order.

As he entered the Master's study he was asked 'Did you notice whereabouts my umbrella was in the hallway as you came in the front door?'.

'No, I didn't,' said the student.

'I'm sorry, but you have failed the test,' said the Master.

It is internal concentration and representations that impair perception and obviously it is not allowed in Zen! We need not go so far, but we do need to be in control in those areas.

The first step in that direction is awareness.

Things are not so different when it comes to behaviour. The same central symptom applies, based on the assumption that our state is not our own creation: that it is something happening to us rather than being something done by us. In fact, of course, we can have as much choice as we decide to choose!

The late R. D. Laing was a famous psychiatrist. He used to tell of a patient who was referred to him because of his   depression.

As soon as the man walked into his London consulting room and said 'Hello', Laing realised that the patient came from the same part of Scotland as himself. The two men found an immediate bond and were soon chatting away, exchanging jokes and anecdotes.

After an hour, the time came to leave and the man got up from his chair still talking and laughing.

As he went to open the door, he suddenly froze and his shoulders drooped. He turned round to Laing with his face creased with deep lines and all the light and sparkle gone out of his eyes. 'But we haven't talked about my depression,' he said in slow mournful tones.

Laing knew exactly what was going on. 'I'm sorry,' he replied briskly, looking at his watch, 'the session is over now.'

'Oh!' said the man snapping out of it immediately and assuming a normal upright posture, 'Oh well, thanks very much then. See you next week'.

All that the great psychotherapist had to do the next week was to run through the sequence with his patient. By understanding what had happened, the man was brought to realise that he could, and indeed did, choose and control his state and therefore his behaviour.

Automatic mechanical behaviour patterns are obviously an obstacle to communication. If both parties in the process are acting on automatic pilot, the result is communication deadlock through incongruity and complete lack of rapport.

Sometimes routine behaviour patterns and sequences can be broken by using a '**pattern interrupt**'. As you may imagine, this means responding to a piece of automatic behaviour in a conspicuously unexpected way.

There are stories about Red Indians being chased by angry grizzly bears. The bears were undoubtedly in an automatic behaviour pattern! Legend has it that the Indians avoided certain death by singing at the creatures or by stopping and standing on their heads. The bears were so nonplussed by this inappropriate reaction that their pattern of aggression was broken for long enough to allow the Indians to get away.

This story might suggest that pattern interruptions are a truly desperate remedy! In human relations they can work, but they need to be used with sensitivity.

If you are trying to have a conversation with someone and you feel they are on automatic pilot, you would certainly break their pattern if you stood on your head and began singing - or even doing something not quite so unexpected. You would certainly get their attention, but we could not guarantee that you would go on from there to reach the result you initially hoped for!

As with Laing's patient, what is important is that we should be able to recognise when we ourselves are drifting into automatic mode.

Once we have made headway in that area, we can move on to helping others and we do not need to discuss any further new techniques for that.

There is an old saying '*If you want to help other people, be prepared to change yourself*'. If we are not clear in ourselves, attempts to help others will only extend our confusion to them. However, once we **are** in the clear ourselves, the way to help others becomes obvious.

The energy which can result from creative communication can be tremendously powerful. It can be the fuel which we use on the journey from where we are now to where we want to be. The response ability in ourselves to be able to recognise and react to the responses of other people is equivalent to spotting and being able to read the signposts along the road. The more information we have, the more accurate our driving becomes. The more accurate our driving is, the more destinations we can reach.

Imagine the latent possibilities in the power of two or more people who are in alignment and rapport in this way! So develop full responsibility and be ready to be flexible in your communications.

    ✰ Build up your sensory acuity.

    ✰ Practise your language skills.

    ✰ Develop your listening skills.

Tune in to all these messages and you will find yourself dealing with any differences of opinion, *elegantly.*

You will be able to manage misunderstandings and disagreements, *elegantly.*

You will discover how to achieve mutually beneficial results from your relationships, once again, of course, *elegantly*!

You will be a Peak Performance Communicator.

A F T E R T H O U G H T

Did you think it was all over?

As we look back over this book, it seems to us that we could easily construct two very different scenarios from what we have outlined.

In the first we would be in the world of 'Average Performance.' The cast of characters live their lives stuck in second gear. They are too frightened to go any faster in case they fall over the edge.

On the one hand, they complain bitterly that they have found no great scriptwriter in the sky, while, at the same time on the other hand, they also complain that they cannot become their own scriptwriters because they are convinced that they have had their second-class parts forced upon them. They are probably right in that conviction, because they behave in automatic mechanistic fashions conditioned by the negative belief systems of the society in which they were brought up.

Except when they are surrounded by people in the same situation, they feel like strangers in a strange land. That challenging world feels vaguely threatening and, under the control of that illusion, it is as much as they can do to get out of bed in the morning! They are haunted by the lack of success or achievement in a past from which they feel they can never escape. For them the future is an unknown and frightening country where they feel they will have no control. They may have some vague hopes. They have no sense of certainty.

Most of their energy is spent clinging to the mast to avoid being torn away from the boat by every wind that blows. Average Performance people are convinced that somebody else should be doing a better job of keeping the boat away from the wind in the first place. Whoever that person is, it certainly is not one of them.

Worst of all for these people is that they cannot even help each other. They have accepted a certain inherited view of things which they remain constantly convinced is a true reflection of the world about them and which they can do nothing to change. When these Average Performers bump into each other they quite unconsciously reinforce their internal images because they see an accurate reflection mirrored in each other's personalities.

Even if they wanted to try to do something to change their defeatist state, they would find it impossible to communicate effectively because of the constant noises of their negative internal dialogue. The only words that slip through in the course of any dialogue are those which are in tune with their own thinking. That can do nothing but support and increase the negativity as it pursues its way around a vicious circle.

The real problem for the future is that these are the concepts and attitudes which they will hand on to their children, which promises little for the prospects of the next generation.

In the alternative world of Peak Performance we have a totally different cast of characters. They live at a rate of smooth acceleration, in full confidence that the world will provide many alternative pathways for them as they move forward. They are prepared to take responsibility for writing their own scripts, behaving in a self-determined and flexible manner. They no longer allow themselves to be controlled by negative belief systems inherited from their society.

The world they see in front of them is full of promise and, guided by that promise, positive action becomes more and more natural and effortless. They can deal with their inherited pasts where they have to. The future offers fresh fields which they approach with curiosity and optimism, with no fear of the unforeseeable opportunities they will offer.

Taking control of their lives with total responsibility, Peak Performers know how to set a better sail when the wind changes direction. They have time to enjoy the view instead of clinging to the mast. Since they are steering the boat themselves, they do not have to worry about where the wind may try to take them. With their own hand on the tiller, they make use of the power of the wind to go where they intend.

They have learned how to create new empowering mental movies which they know how to control. As a result, when they meet other Peak Performers, they do not view each other through any distorting lenses. They can see each other clearly. They hear each other clearly too, for they have the time, the patience and the skill to listen effectively. Their language is positive and, with all the other skill materials, creates the virtuous circle of positive feed-back.

The prospects which they hand on to their children are crafted by the positive tool-kit which we have described. Of course those prospects will include the freedom to choose for themselves and to weigh and balance any inherited beliefs which may be offered until that next generation make up their own minds. We hope that they will have chosen both freedom and responsibility for themselves.

Which world are you going to choose to live in? Average Performance or Peak Performance? Right at the beginning of this book we asked another question - *'Who do you think you are?'*

In many ways both these questions may seem to be rhetorical, and yet, as you think about this latest simple question, it is possible that your old thought patterns may be asking yet another question at the back of your mind. *'What is it going to cost me?'*

The answer to that question is simple. **Everything!**

What is more it is payable in advance. You cannot buy into this by instalments. Is that fair enough?

 We believe so, absolutely. We think it is even better than fair. It is ultimately desirable and should be irresistible. We are talking about total commitment which is what we are designed for.

Is anyone still feeling doubtful out there? What we say is, think about it. Decide if you would really prefer your future any other way. It is our destiny to fulfil our potential and human beings are never truly happy, no matter what they may say, unless they are fully stretched and dealing with the greatest challenges that they are each personally capable of meeting.

Living below that level results in feelings of dissatisfaction and demoralisation which dampen any enthusiasm and dull our outlook.

The commitment to fulfil our potential is what makes Peak Performers. We all know that, if we stop to listen for it, we can hear a voice pushing us to make this journey. That voice in each of us is life demanding just as much as we can deal with. At times most of us have experienced periods of time when the demands slackened off for a while. Think of those long school holidays. Very often they were fun to begin with, but equally often we became bored and were ready to welcome even the prospect of getting back to school!

If you have heard the promptings of that inner voice telling you to get on with the journey and you have not followed its directions, you are going to find yourself dissatisfied with what you have made of your life so far. You feel a longing for something more, a step further. That is your potential knocking on the door which you have locked and demanding to be let out.

Have you ever deliberately ignored those inner promptings and allowed yourself to drift on without direction? Most of us have at sometime. That probably includes you. Perhaps you have felt comfortable and unchallenged for a while, but sooner or later that changes and you become demoralised.

The only way to overcome boredom and demoralisation is to make the decision and go for it. When you do, the force from within and the force from without are acknowledged and focused into a single vision directed by your own personal leadership. All the underlying energies of life are ignited and your great adventure is launched and leaps into existence.

As we come near the end of this book, we do so with the positive presumption that you would not have come this far if you were not ready to make the commitment. So it is time to take a final look at the checklist.

Exercise 26   Check for Balance

* You have assembled all the necessary materials to design your own future.
* You have mastered all the behaviours and skills from the Peak Performance programme.
* You have assumed the responsibility of personal leadership bringing all those elements into alignment.
* You conduct your own orchestra.
* Your behaviour moves you towards your goals because of your beliefs.
* Your beliefs serve your values which support your personal vision.
* Your personal freedom grows daily.
* Your choice of responses grows daily because you are no longer on automatic pilot.
* Your choice of responses increases your opportunities.

As you tick off all those items on the checklist, you realise that you have a finely tuned vehicle to accelerate into the future as you keep the wheel of life in balance.

You have learned if you only want to **know** what you are going to be, all you have to do is look at where and what you are now.

On the other hand if you want to **decide** who and what you are going to be, you only have to take control. The vehicle is yours; drive it forward smoothly, effectively and without hesitation. We all have the capacity to design and realise our own destinies.

'What the mind of man can conceive, the will of man can achieve.'

The power lies within ourselves. It is not in our personal histories. It is not in society. It is not in our environment. It is in ourselves as we are today.

This is something that is easy to do and equally easy not to do! Just make up your mind to be one of those who decide to do it. To quote Napoleon Hill, '*Cut yourself away from the average and the mediocre, and chart yourself on the dream in your heart!*'

Accept that challenge.

Take action.

Take massive action.

Become a Peak Performer.

Do it now!

HE BROKE THROUGH

ALADDIN AND THE GENIE

Aladdin, having seen the film, was not all that surprised when the Genie appeared. What did surprise him was being offered only one wish.

'Wait a minute,' he protested. 'I thought people always got three wishes.'

'Yes, but they always wasted the first two,' said the Genie. 'Anyway, our research indicated that people only need one wish granted, providing they wish for the right thing.'

'Which is?'

'The wish to free themselves from their own conditioning and to give themselves the power to choose their own behaviours. You see, this situation we're in is really metaphorical. What you need to realise is that in actual fact you yourself are a Genie. You already have all the magic you need. So I strongly advise you to ask for the freedom to use it.'

'Oh,' said Aladdin, thinking it over, 'but in the film the last wish was for your freedom, not mine.'

'Don't worry about that,' said the Genie, 'that's already sorted.'

Well, Aladdin asked for his freedom and was heading off into the sunset when a sudden thought made him return to ask a question. He found the Genie packing up his gear.

'Hang on a minute,' he said, 'if we're all our own Genie then how come you have to go around doing all this stuff?'

'Good question,' said the Genie, 'in the first place, I don't have to do it. It's something I choose to do. Most of us need a nudge before we take ownership of our own magic and choose our own freedom. That's what a Genie is for. I met my own Genie a long time ago, and claimed my own freedom. Helping other people claim their freedom is what I chose to do with my freedom.'

'You mean you're . . . ?'

'That's right,' said the Genie, 'I'm a Peak Performance coach!'

D
edicated to making a difference in the corporate world, Speakers International advocates the development of high performance individuals, teams and organisations. Their approach combines a high level of business awareness with a dynamic and entertaining delivery style.

They understand that the most effective way of acquiring and applying knowledge, is not only to create an interest but to deliver the information in a way that empowers people to take action. All of their programmes incorporate cutting edge strategies making their programmes and presentations highly interactive, participative and most of all fun.

Jim Steele, Martin Coburn and Colin Hiles of Speakers International Corporate Development Ltd have all developed the Breakthrough to Peak Performance Programme.

Breakthrough to Peak Performance programmes aim to coach people to release the potential within them. Whether you are in business, education or sport we have programmes to suit your needs. Join us on one of our Open Programmes or book a Programme for your whole team.

** Mastering Your Motivation **

Understand the principles and strategies that create peak performance in business or sport and how to apply them consistently to create excellence.

** The Power of Belief **

Henry Ford said 'Whether you think you can or think you can't, you're probably right'. Create tangible results through understanding the power of beliefs in achieving desired outcomes.

** Personal Leadership in Action **

Explore the strategies used by the world's top performers and become a self-acting person who takes responsibility and is self-led.

** Effective Communications **

Enhance your flexibility and effectiveness in communicating with others.

** Impact – Power Presentations **

Powerful presenters are impactful and their messages compelling. Watch how your own ability to make an impact grows as you learn these strategies.

** Coaching for Peak Performance **

How to get optimum performance out of individuals and in turn create winning teams.

For more information about the authors, Speakers International Corporate Development Ltd and their coaching programmes please contact them at:

Speakers International Corporate Development Ltd,
4 Berghem Mews, Blythe Road,
London W14 0HN
Tel: 0171 602 9498 Fax: 0171 602 9101
http\\:www:speakers-international.com or
email **speakers@speakers-international.com.**

P U B L I S H E R ' S

P O S T S C R I P T

Nowadays, more and more people are seeking for a pathway that leads to personal inner satisfaction. Different people call it by different names. You will hear them speak of Personal Development, Personal Growth, Self-Development, Self-Actualization, New Age Thought and many others.

At the beginning of the 1990's, Peter Russell, in his book 'The Awakening Earth', estimated that the field of personal development was a growing area which was doubling roughly every four years. Things have accelerated since then, and as we near the end of the decade it is obvious that the rate of development has increased. In its widest sense, Personal Development covers a broad range of activities including rebirthing, assertiveness training, prosperity consciousness and transactional analysis, neuro-linguistic programming and associated techniques such as yoga, tai chi, acupuncture, hypnotherapy, meditation and Gestalt therapy.

At the end of this postscript we list a brief bibliography of works in these varied areas which will help you take steps along whichever path you may have chosen.

Before you go any further down this path which you have decided to follow, pause and reflect on the fact that whatever decisions you make and whichever paths you choose to take, it will involve an investment of time and money. It may involve organising and travelling, buying books and tapes, doing courses or attending training seminars.

It is worth taking a few moments to work out roughly what percentage of your income you have invested in developing yourself over the last few years.

Begin by making a list of what you would count as personal development activities in your life as opposed to other things such as entertainment. The difference should not be too difficult to spot! The first kind make a permanent difference in your life. The second kind do not. It is the difference between, for example, a training course or planned meditation on the one hand, which would be the first kind and, on the other hand, going out for a special meal or whatever other kind of entertainment you might choose, which would be the second.

Now make a rough estimate of the financial costs of these activities. Notice also the benefits you might have gained from each. Compare the two costs. What percentage of your total income does each amount to?

It is worth comparing this percentage to the proportion of income which **Companies** spend on training and developing their people. For some that may be as little as one or two percent. Increasingly, and for the most successful companies, the figure rises to something closer to ten percent.

The percentage of your income that you are prepared to invest in yourself is a reflection of how much you value yourself.

Remember, you are your own most valuable asset and resource. '**Me Ltd**' is the best organisation to invest in.

If you are involved in a Company or Organisation which believes in the value of training and you understand the significance of what we are saying, the address to contact for further information is:-

Speakers International Corporate Development Ltd.

4 Berghem Mews

Blythe Road

LONDON   W14 0HN

http//:www.speakers-international.com

(0171 602 9498)

All the books in the following bibliography may be obtained from:-

The Catalyst Group

1 Berghem Mews

Blythe Road

LONDON   W14 0HN

(0171 603 7779)

Catalyst is a leading publisher and distributor of books, audio tapes and videos, specialising in high quality personal development titles.

Should you require a wider selection in any particular field, Catalyst catalogues may be obtained from the same address. Most Catalyst books and audio programs are available at significant discounts when purchased in bulk.

Further information and a complete bookshop can be found at:

http//:www.catayst-group.com

Bibliography follows.

263

BIBLIOGRAPHY

Awaken the Giant Within — Anthony Robbins

Being Happy — Andrew Matthews

Feel the Fear and Do it Anyway — Susan Jeffers

Instant Rapport — Michael Brooks

Introducing NLP — O'Connor/Seymour

The Magic of Thinking Big — David Schwartz

Maximum Achievement — Brian Tracy

NLP at Work — Sue Knight

Seven Habits of Highly Effective People — Stephen Covey

Seven Strategies for Wealth and Happiness — Jim Rohn

Unlimited Power — Anthony Robbins

A P P E N D I X

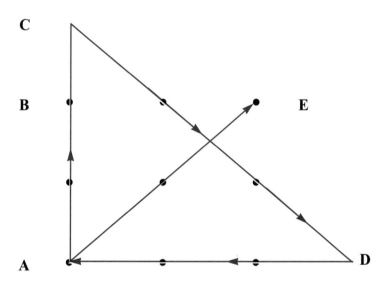

This is our solution to the 'nine dots' problem.

Begin at point **A** and travel to **B**, then carry on for half that distance further. Now, change direction and follow the arrow to the point **D** which you can see is also outside the square formed by the original nine dots. Again follow the arrow and return to **A**. Now change direction for the last time and pick up the last two dots as you move to **E**.

The solution is easy when you know how! The important thing is that knowing how means realising that you have to be prepared to go outside the framework suggested to you by the nine dots when you first looked at them. There was nothing in the rules of the challenge to say that you could not do this.

Anytime you find yourself faced by a problem which appears to have no solution, ask yourself about the implied 'rules' which you are accepting, which seem to make the situation impossible. Once you have identified those rules, you may find yourself in a new and more empowered situation. You may be able to change what you assumed were fixed parameters, and, in this way, a new approach may allow you to find a way to solve your insoluble problem!

Ordering More Peak Perfomance....

You may order more copies of this book for a limited time at pre-publication discounts:

Single Copy	£19.99
10+ Copies	£17.99
25+ Copies	£15.99
100+ Copies	£13.95

Special price quotes available for orders of 1,000 or more.

Please send me_____ copies of the book at £___ a copy. (plus postage and packing)

Credit Card: Amex/Diners/Visa/Mastercard:

Card No:_____ Expires_____

Please Print Your Name, Title, Company and Address Clearly:

Name:_____Title:_____

Company:_____

Address:_____

_____

_____Postcode_____

Tel:_____Fax:_____

PHONE OR FAX YOUR ORDER TO CATALYST ON:
Tel: +44 (0)171 603 7779 Fax: +44 (0)171 603 2220